INSPIRE / PLAN / DISCOVER / EXPERIENCE

NEW ORLEANS

NEW ORLEANS

CONTENTS

DISCOVER 6

EXPERIENCE 56

NEED TO KNOW 200

Left: Brass band performing at a parade
Previous page: City skyline seen from the Mississippi
Front cover: Colorful French Quarter buildings

DISCOVER

The CBD skyline, illuminated at dusk

WELCOME TO
NEW ORLEANS

Nowhere in the United States is quite like New Orleans. This is the "Crescent City," set in a sultry curve of the Mississippi River, where a history of strong European, Caribbean, and African influences have shaped a local culture like no other. This heady mix results in a daily celebration of life, reflected in the city's food, music, and many traditions. Whatever your dream trip to New Orleans includes, this DK Eyewitness Travel Guide is the perfect companion.

1 A red streetcar clattering along Canal Street.

2 Admiring a mansion in the leafy Garden District.

3 Fresh boiled crawfish, a Louisiana specialty.

4 Gathering around a brass band on Frenchmen.

Trundle through town aboard the famous streetcar and watch 300 years of history unfurl. From Gothic mansions, through colorful Creole cottages, to the elegant wrought-iron galleries of the French Quarter, the city's historic architecture creates a stunning cinematic backdrop.

Art is everywhere. Immerse yourself in Louisiana's finest at the Ogden Museum of Southern Art, and get lost in NOMA's dazzling array of international treasures. The food scene is equally enticing, with everything from Cajun crawfish to Vietnamese bánh mi on the menu, accompanied by a classic cocktail, of course.

This generous party city is also known as the "Big Easy," and its Mardi Gras spirit lives on year-round in jubilant daily celebrations and raucous nightly revelry on Bourbon Street. And don't forget, this is the home of jazz. Streets resound with a cacophony of music, from the buzz of cool clubs on Frenchmen, to the brassy bursts of Second Lines marching through Treme.

If it all gets too much, head to the river and catch a breeze cruising along on a paddlesteamer. Outside the city, the landscape unfolds into watery Cajun swamps and bayous, where boat trips drift through mossy stands of cypress.

So, where to start? We've broken the city down into easily navigable chapters, with detailed itineraries, expert local knowledge, and colorful, comprehensive maps to help you plan the perfect visit. Whether you're staying for a weekend, a week, or longer, this Eyewitness guide will ensure that you see the very best New Orleans has to offer. Enjoy the book, and enjoy New Orleans.

REASONS TO LOVE
NEW ORLEANS

Infectious music, irresistible food, the beauty of the Mississippi, historic neighborhoods, and the world's biggest free party, Mardi Gras. There are endless reasons to love New Orleans, but here are some of our favorites.

1 LIVE JAZZ
This is the birthplace of jazz, and you can't leave the city without experiencing the scene *(p28)*. Preservation Hall is the spot to hear traditional bands play every night *(p77)*.

GREEN PARKS 2
With vast City Park in the north *(p176)*, riverside Crescent Park in the east *(p119)*, and bucolic Audubon Park to the west *(p156)*, New Orleans is a truly green and pleasant city.

3 SIPPING ON CLASSIC COCKTAILS
A special kind of alchemy gives rise to the city's classic tipples. Brandy milk punch at brunch, or a sazerac at sundown, any time is the right time to savor a classic New Orleans cocktail.

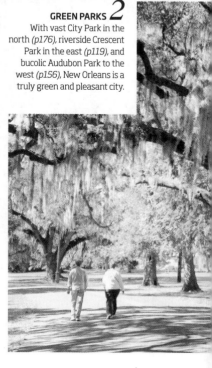

LGBT+ CULTURE 4
NOLA is a liberal island in the state of Louisiana, with LGBT+ bars and clubs filling the French Quarter, and Pride and Southern Decadence festival dominating the calendar *(p46)*.

THE FESTIVALS 5
New Orleans' calendar is packed with celebrations of its culture *(p46)*. Joining Mardi Gras are legendary music festivals like Jazz Fest *(p172)*, and jubilant daily parades *(p114)*.

DIVERSE CULTURES 6
A gumbo of international influences are evident in the culture of this eclectic place, from its colorful Creole cottages to the ubiquitous Italian-inspired muffuletta sandwich.

MARDI GRAS 7

New Orleans comes alive during a month of parades and parties. This culminates on Mardi Gras day, when the entire city dons fancy dress in a cacophony of revelry *(p66)*.

WANDERING THE FRENCH QUARTER 8

The city's 300-year-old heart will awaken your inner *flaneur (p58)*. Here, elegant ironwork-galleried streets are lined with antique stores, lively, storied bars, and Creole dining rooms.

9 RIDING THE ST. CHARLES STREETCAR

Hop on the iconic green streetcar and trundle slowly uptown, past university campuses and opulent mansions along one of the city's most beautiful avenues *(p142)*.

10 TASTING CLASSIC LOCAL FOODS

Creole, Cajun, Caribbean, and European influences mean unique New Orleanian delicacies to suit every taste, from gumbo and jambalaya, to po'boys and beignets *(p26)*.

11 THE MISSISSIPPI

The river is a symbol of the city, and the source of its identity. Steamboat *Natchez* offers gentle jazz cruises *(p74)*, and Moon Walk is perfect for waterside strolling *(p98)*.

12 SHOPPING

Window shoppers and big spenders rejoice *(p38)*. Try Royal St. for antiques, Magazine St. for boutiques, or the Warehouse District for unbeatable fine art.

EXPLORE
NEW ORLEANS

This guide divides New Orleans into six color-coded sightseeing areas, as shown on this map. Find out more about each area on the following pages. For sights beyond the city center, see p180.

City Park

Greenwood Cemetery

Metairie Cemetery

PONTCHARTRAIN EXPRESSWAY

CANAL STREET

ORLEANS

MID-CITY
p162

TULANE AVENUE

AIRLINE DRIVE

EARHART EXPRESSWAY

HOLLYGROVE

MONTICELLO AVENUE

CARROLLTON AVENUE

WASHINGTON AVENUE

SOUTHPORT

CARROLLTON

RIVERBEND

BROADMOOR

CLAIBORNE AVENUE

RIVER ROAD

UNIVERSITY DISTRICT

BROADWAY

AVENUE

LOUISIANA

GARDEN DISTRICT AND UPTOWN
p138

Audubon Park

Audubon Zoo

JEFFERSON

ST CHARLES AVENUE

MAGAZINE STREET

TCHOUPITOULAS STREET

IRISH CHANNEL

Mississippi

RIVER ROAD

WESTBANK EXPRESSWAY

WESTWEGO

4TH STREET

MARRERO

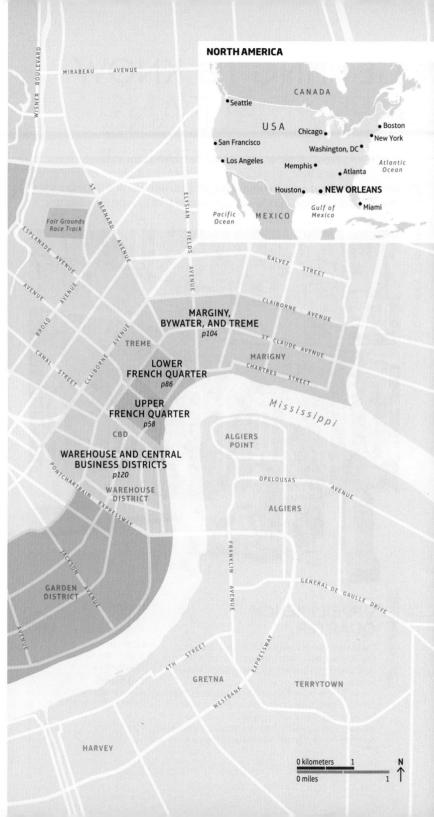

NORTH AMERICA

CANADA

USA

- Seattle
- Chicago
- Boston
- New York
- San Francisco
- Washington, DC
- Los Angeles
- Memphis
- Atlanta
- Houston
- **NEW ORLEANS**
- Miami

Atlantic Ocean

Pacific Ocean

MEXICO

Gulf of Mexico

WISNER BOULEVARD

MIRABEAU AVENUE

ST BERNARD AVENUE

ELYSIAN FIELDS AVENUE

Fair Grounds Race Track

ESPLANADE AVENUE

AVENUE

BROAD AVENUE

CLAIBORNE AVENUE

CANAL STREET

GALVEZ STREET

CLAIBORNE AVENUE

TREME

MARGINY, BYWATER, AND TREME
p104

ST CLAUDE AVENUE

MARIGNY

CHARTRES STREET

LOWER FRENCH QUARTER
p86

Mississippi

UPPER FRENCH QUARTER
p58

CBD

ALGIERS POINT

WAREHOUSE AND CENTRAL BUSINESS DISTRICTS
p120

WAREHOUSE DISTRICT

PONTCHARTRAIN EXPRESSWAY

OPELOUSAS AVENUE

ALGIERS

JACKSON AVENUE

FRANKLIN AVENUE

GENERAL DE GAULLE DRIVE

GARDEN DISTRICT

AVENUE

4TH STREET

WESTBANK EXPRESSWAY

GRETNA

TERRYTOWN

HARVEY

0 kilometers 1
0 miles 1

N

GETTING TO KNOW
NEW ORLEANS

The famous French Quarter, with its ornate architecture and joyful music, is the city's historic heart. But winding along the Mississippi are colorful neighborhoods with superb museums, intriguing cemeteries, and landmark sites to explore, as well as Cajun towns and swamplands beyond New Orleans.

PAGE 58

UPPER FRENCH QUARTER

The city grew around Jackson Square, and this part of the French Quarter is home to some of its most iconic sights. From the Dixieland jazz ringing out from street corners, to the delicious aromas of spicy Cajun and Creole dishes wafting from cafés and restaurants, this densely packed network of historic streets is a feast for the senses. Take a walk down Royal Street, where antique stores glow with glittering treasures, and wander along Bourbon Street to let the good times roll.

Best for
Sightseeing, fine dining, and strolling along the river

Home to
St. Louis Cathedral, The Historic New Orleans Collection

Experience
A cruise along the Mississippi aboard the Steamboat Natchez

LOWER FRENCH QUARTER

PAGE 86

The bustling French Market aside, this is the quieter end of the French Quarter, its tranquil residential streets offering a calm escape from the crowds. Here, classic New Orleans architecture of Creole cottages sit neatly alongside some of the city's oldest buildings like the Old Ursuline Convent. Historic mansions such as Gallier House now hold museums offering an insight into what life was like in times gone by.

Best for
Admiring ironwork architecture and historic houses

Home to
The French Market

Experience
Tasting sugar-dusted beignets with coffee at Café du Monde

PAGE 104

MARIGNY, BYWATER, AND TREME

Treme is the country's oldest African American neighborhood, and here its spirit and culture bubbles up from the streets, with jubilant brass bands marching through the district. Downriver, Marigny and Bywater are peppered with colorful shotgun houses and Creole cottages, as well as spectacular street murals. Linger and soak up the atmosphere of second-hand stores, art galleries, and hip cafés, and cycle along the serene riverfront in Crescent Park. These quarters come alive at night, trendy Bywater eateries throng with diners, and revellers spill out from the jazz clubs of cool musical enclave, Frenchmen Street.

Best for
Jazz clubs, African American history

Home to
St. Louis Cemetery #1, Louis Armstrong Park

Experience
Jazz-bar-hopping on Frenchmen Street

$\rightarrow$

WAREHOUSE AND CENTRAL BUSINESS DISTRICTS

The broad thoroughfare of Canal Street marks the start of the city's commercial center. But the Central Business District is much more than a corporate corridor. Beneath the bright lights of the Superdome, sophisticated bars and restaurants vie with landmark theaters and luxury shopping spots. The adjoining Warehouse District has been reborn as the city's Arts District, the SoHo of the South. This area glows with lively creativity, with its clutch of vibrant galleries alongside outstanding museums.

Best for
Museums and art galleries, shopping

Home to
Audubon Aquarium of the Americas

Experience
Diving into Louisiana's art at the Ogden Museum of Southern Art

GARDEN DISTRICT AND UPTOWN

A ride on the clattering St. Charles Avenue Streetcar transports you to the city's leafiest district. Wander past grand, eclectic mansions and explore tranquil Lafayette Cemetery; a stroll here seems a world away from the bustling city center. Uptown you'll find prestigious universities and family fun in Audubon Park, along with trendy Magazine Street, home to independent boutiques and cool cafés.

Best for
Grand historic homes, ornate cemeteries

Home to
St. Charles Avenue Streetcar, Audubon Zoo

Experience
Riding the streetcar along St. Charles Avenue

MID-CITY

PAGE 162

Dominating this district is City Park, a vast oasis of parkland cut through by a tangle of bayous and lagoons. Ride the classic wooden carousel with the kids in Storyland, or wander the lush grounds of the New Orleans Botanical Garden. The park is also home to the outstanding New Orleans Museum of Art (NOMA) and the expansive Besthoff Sculpture Garden. Along the park's eastern edge is Bayou St. John, an inner-city creek that winds northwards to Lake Pontchartrain. The bayou's grassy banks provide a picturesque spot for picnics, parties, and the occasional crawfish boil.

Best for
Art galleries and picnic spots

Home to
New Orleans Museum of Art

Experience
Relaxing beneath the live oaks in City Park

BEYOND NEW ORLEANS

PAGE 180

New Orleans' surroundings provide a vertiginous contrast to its compact city center. Just a few hours' drive away is the River Road, where former plantation mansions, now museums, give visitors a taste of antebellum life. Further west lie the massive Atchafalaya Swamp and sprawling Cajun Country, where Francophone culture awaits in Lafayette's robust, spicy cuisine, and lively music scene. Meanwhile to the north, the Louisiana state capital of Baton Rouge is a thriving metropolis, with a vibrant nightlife and historic attractions.

Best for
Museums, Cajun culture

Home to
The Whitney Plantation, Lafayette, Baton Rouge

Experience
Spotting alligators on a swamp tour

←

1 Admiring artworks in Jackson Square.

2 Café du Monde.

3 Cruising along the river aboard Steamboat *Natchez*.

4 The neon lights of busy Bourbon Street.

With its romantic architecture, delectable cuisine, and vibrant array of live music and entertainment, New Orleans is a treasure trove for travelers. These itineraries will help you to make the most of your visit.

24 HOURS
in New Orleans

▌ *Morning*

Start by snagging an outdoor table at Café du Monde (p96), New Orleans' landmark coffeehouse. Sink your teeth into soft, powdery beignets and sip hot, chicory coffee as you watch the world go by. Set up for the day, climb the steps to the adjoining Washington Artillery Park for a splendid panoramic view over Jackson Square (p76), flanked by the handsome Pontalba Buildings (p77) and the impressive trio from the early French and Spanish colony: St. Louis Cathedral (p62), the Presbytère (p64), and the Cabildo (p68). Wander the lively square, enjoying the tunes of jazz musicians, and watch artists displaying their colorful paintings on the perimeter fence. Head up nearby Pirate's Alley (p79) to Royal Street (p70). Take a left to reach the Historic New Orleans Collection and spend an hour here ogling the paintings and rich decorative arts (p72). Then stroll back along Royal Street, to admire beautifully preserved, traditional architecture, and pop into art galleries and antique shops filled with glittering treasures.

▌ *Afternoon*

By now you'll have worked up an appetite, so wander along Decatur Street to reach the Central Grocery (p96). Indulge in a classic muffuletta sandwich stuffed with tasty Italian deli meats, cheese, and olive salad – you can take it away to tuck in at the little park across the street beneath a golden Joan of Arc statue. Tummy full, head to the riverfront to board the iconic Steamboat *Natchez* – you'll recognize the peals of the boat's calliope organ from a mile away (p74). Put your feet up on a relaxing two-hour river cruise (departing at 2.30pm), accompanied by live jazz, fascinating narratives on the city, and breezy views of the busy waterway.

▌ *Evening*

Back on dry land, it's nearly cocktail time, so make your way to Bourbon Street, where there are lively bars to suit every style (p77). Start at the Old Absinthe House (p81). Oozing historic atmosphere, this has been a French Quarter watering hole since 1807. Then sip a sundowner at the elegant Arnaud's French 75 Bar, named after its classy champagne cocktail (p81). For fans of Tennessee Williams' play *A Streetcar Named Desire*, Galatoire's makes the perfect choice for dinner, with its delicious traditional Creole cuisine (p77). Your last port of call is Frenchmen Street, to party the night away in laid-back jazz clubs (p117).

←

[1] The French Market.

[2] An elegant lunch at Ralph's on the Park.

[3] Music and dancing at the Spotted Cat on Frenchmen.

[4] Bright lights of the grand Saenger Theatre.

3 DAYS
in New Orleans

Day 1

Morning Beat the crowds with an early start at the French Market (p90). Breakfast is coffee and a pastry from the food stalls, followed by a wander through the busy flea market. When you've picked up some souvenirs, aim for Jackson Square (p76) where you'll peak inside St. Louis Cathedral to glimpse the beautifully carved Baroque altar (p62).

Afternoon For lunch, stop by Mister Gregory's (p93) and savor a slice of King Cake accompanied by views from the café balcony. Refreshed, hop on the Esplanade Avenue bus to Mid-City for a walk along the tranquil Bayou St. John (p173). Cross Magnolia Bridge to reach the New Orleans Museum of Art, and the vast Besthoff Sculpture Gardens surrounding the museum (p167).

Evening Enjoy a light supper of fresh, farm-to-table fare at Ralph's on the Park (p171). Take the Canal Streetcar back to your hotel, the chic Audubon Cottages (p78), to freshen up for the evening. Then head to the plush Sazerac Bar (p135) for a nightcap of New Orleans' signature rye whiskey cocktail.

Day 2

Morning After breakfast at your hotel, ride the St. Charles Avenue Streetcar to the Garden District (p142). Stroll the leafy streets and admire grand mansions such as Gothic Revival Briggs-Staub House and Greek-columned Robinson House (p147), before exploring the wide avenues of elaborate stone mausoleums in walled Lafayette Cemetery (p146).

Afternoon Take a stroll down Magazine Street and dip into trendy boutiques (p39), before stopping in at Joey K's for a taste of homestyle Creole cooking (joeyks restaurant.com). Reboard the streetcar and continue uptown to Audubon Zoo, home to rare and endangered creatures from around the globe (p144).

Evening Ride the streetcar back to the Warehouse District in time for a contemporary Carribean dinner at Compère Lapin (p129). Take a cab to the Spotted Cat on Frenchmen for late-night jazz (p117).

Day 3

Morning Start the day with a bang-up breakfast at the Ruby Slipper Cafe (the rubyslippercafe.net), before spending a few hours in the huge National WWII Museum touring numerous impressive military displays (p126). Grab a light lunch at the museum café, Jeri Nims Soda Shop.

Afternoon Catch a fresh breeze with a walk along the Mississippi. Wander through Woldenberg Riverfront Park (p128), with its sculptures and gardens, and take a seat on the water's edge to watch the boats go by.

Evening Suitably chilled out, head to modern Cajun restaurant Cochon for an early dinner of fine charcuterie and a glass or two of old-world wine (p129). Then make for the beautiful Italianate Saenger Theatre and end your day with a spectacular Broadway show (p133).

5 DAYS

Day 1

Morning Set out first thing for a wander of Jackson Square *(p76)* – you'll beat the crowds, and catch the morning light accenting the square's lacey ironwork. Peek into the Presbytère *(p64)*, where you can ease into a morning yoga session run by Friends of the Cabildo *(p69)*.

Afternoon Begin an afternoon of French Quarter strolling with lunch at Coop's Place *(p93)*. Then pay a visit to nearby Gallier Historic House and Soniat House museums, for a glimpse of life in the 19th century *(p94)*.

Evening Have dinner in the courtyard of a charming Creole cottage at Bayona, before catching a show at Bourbon Street jazz club Fritzel's *(p77)*. Stay up late at nearby Old Absinthe House *(p81)*.

Day 2

Morning Make your way to Treme to immerse yourself in the rich African American history of this district. Meander through Louis Armstrong Park *(p108)* taking in the sculptures of Congo Square, before lingering in the Backstreet Cultural Museum, to learn about Mardi Gras traditions *(p115)*.

Afternoon Dip into sleek Meauxbar bistro for a light lunch *(p94)*, and then follow a guided tour of St. Louis #1 Cemetery *(p112)*, led by Two Chicks Walking Tours *(twochickswalkingtours.com)*.

Evening For dinner, make for famed Dooky Chase and savor classic Creole dishes of gumbo and shrimp *clemenceau* *(p171)*. Return to the French Quarter, and while the night away listening to impeccable trad jazz at Preservation Hall *(p77)*.

Day 3

Morning Have a hearty breakfast at Buffa's, ready for a day of cycling *(buffas restaurant.com)*. Rent a Blue Bike *(p207)* and ride through Marigny and Bywater, past colorful Creole cottages and shotgun houses. Continue along the river through Crescent Park *(p119)*, and stop at Pizza Delicious for the best slice in town *(p118)*.

1. Wandering Jackson Square.

2. Trad jazz performance at legendary Preservation Hall.

3. Tasty small plates at Shaya.

4. Cocktail at Hot Tin rooftop bar.

5. Cycling through City Park.

6. The Audubon Aquarium of the Americas.

Afternoon Head north to roll along the Lafitte Greenway and continue on up to City Park where you'll wheel past lagoons and groves of oak trees *(p176)*.

Evening After leaving your bike at one of the many Blue Bike stands across the city, head to Magazine Street. Take it easy with a cold beer or two at the Bulldog *(bulldog.draftfreak.com)*, then hop in a cab to nearby Shaya for a dinner of modern Israeli cuisine *(p147)*.

Day 4

Morning Start early and hit the espresso bar at Tout La, in the lobby of the Old 77 Hotel *(p133)*. After coffee and pastries, head over to the Audubon Aquarium of the Americas where astonishing displays of underwater worlds await *(p124)*.

Afternoon Amble along the riverfront to the Outlet Collection at Riverwalk for souvenirs and lunch inside the mall *(p129)*. Ride the ferry across the river to Algiers Point and back, taking in the sparkling city vistas *(p128)*.

Evening After a luxurious Cajun Creole dinner at Emeril's *(p129)*, spend the evening dipping in and out of the dozens of art galleries along Julia Street *(p136)*.

Day 5

Morning Rise early to get to the Jean Lafitte National Historical Park Visitor Center in time for the 9.30am ranger talk *(p81)*. After delving into the geography of the Mississippi River Delta, drop into Verti Marte and pick up a lunchtime po'boy sandwich *(p93)*.

Afternoon Head back to your hotel in time for the afternoon pick-up for a Barataria Preserve swamp tour *(p194)*. Out in the reserve, you'll spot alligators, turtles, and pelicans as you glide through a lattice of cypress-lined bayous by boat.

Evening Shake off the swamp and head to The Joint for a supper of slow-cooked barbecue *(p118)*. Take a cab across town to the Pontchartrain Hotel *(p148)* where you'll savor cocktails and superb skyline vistas at the Hot Tin rooftop bar.

Sweet Treats

Indulge your sweet tooth with New Orleans' decadent desserts. The beignet – a sugar-dusted choux pastry doughnut – is a sweet staple, best savored with coffee at legendary Café du Monde *(p96)*. During Mardi Gras, don't miss out on King Cake, a huge cinnamon pastry roll with carnival-colored frosting. Mister Gregory's makes some of the best cake in town *(p93)*.

←

Café du Monde's famous beignets with hot chicory coffee

NEW ORLEANS FOR
FOODIES

New Orleanians have a generous appetite and a varied palate, and there is a dizzying array of dining options in this city. Cajun and Creole menus dominate, and though New Orleans is marinated in its own gastronomic traditions, there's innovation to explore beyond the classics.

Fine Dining

There are plenty of opulent spots here to satisfy discerning gourmands. Try Galatoire's for turtle soup and duck *andouille (p77)*, or Commander's Palace for its elegant Jazz Brunch and famous 25 cent Martini *(p147)*. Look beyond tradition to the city's cool contemporary spots: Compère Lapin brings a modern twist to Creole and Carribbean cuisine *(p129)*, and new-wave Restaurant R'Evolution breathes new life into the classics with its unique dishes like deconstructed gumbo *(p77)*.

→

Innovative upscale dining at acclaimed Compère Lapin

Comfort Food

From silky Creole gumbo to sustaining Vietnamese pho, New Orleans' comfort food soothes the soul and sates the stomach. Dive into classic Creole cuisine at the city's must-stop soul-food spots. At legendary Dooky Chase savor plates of the most unctuous fried chicken and rich traditional gumbo *(p171)*, or at Coop's Place try the delicately spiced jambalaya *(p93)*. Contemporary Vietnamese restaurant Pho Tau *(www.photaubayres taurant.com)* is the place to slurp on a steaming bowl of pho (noodle soup).

↑ A bowl of rich Creole gumbo, with shrimp, sausage, and okra

Slices of Life

New Orleans is a city of three sandwiches. At Parkway Tavern *(p171)* the homegrown specialty, the mighty po'boy, comes laden with Gulf oyster, shrimp, or roast beef and gravy. Meanwhile, the pillowy Italian-inspired muffaletta is best sampled at Central Grocery *(p94)*. The crisp bánh mì completes the trio – make for Banh Mi Boys to taste this Vietnamese delicacy *(www.bmbmetairie.com)*.

← Local specialty, the muffaletta, filled with cheese and sliced meats

Stuck in Your Craw

A Louisiana specialty, crayfish, crawfish, or mudbugs are lobster-like critters that thrive in freshwater bayous surrounding the city. They're cooked up in a spicy Cajun seasoning with sausages, potatoes, and corn at huge communal "boils" – the perfect occasion to tuck in and socialize. Spots like Royal Street's R Bar *(royalstreet inn.com)* run one boil a week during peak season (March to June). Make sure to seek out this spicy seafood at foodie festivals like Jazzfest *(p172)*.

→

Enjoying spicy Cajun crawfish at a communal boil

Best of the Fests

Mardi Gras promises the city's biggest knees-up *(p66)*, but there are plenty of parties here all year. In Spring, Jazz Fest celebrates jazz, food, and culture *(p172)*, and French Quarter Fest turns the Vieux Carré into a block party showcasing Louisiana's musical heritage *(frenchquarterfest.org)*. Summer's Essence Fest celebrates African American culture with stellar line-ups of RnB and soul artists *(www.essence.com)*.

→

Mary J. Blige performing at Essence Fest

NEW ORLEANS FOR

MUSIC

New Orleans is the birthplace of jazz, but here all genres thrive, with live music suffusing the city with blues, bounce, hip-hop, and soul. From late-night brass band joints to uproarious festivals – in the Big Easy, music lovers are spoilt for choice.

All That Jazz

Think of New Orleans' music, and jazz is the first thing that comes to mind *(p110)*. The city's musical heritage is kept alive at a host of venerable venues. Make for Preservation Hall to enjoy live trad jazz performances every evening *(p77)*. Idle away a night on Bourbon Street at Fritzel's – the city's oldest club – and Jazz Playhouse, which showcases up-and-coming acts *(www.sonesta.com)*. Just a few blocks east, wander along club-lined Frenchmen Street and take in a show for the price of a drink at the bar *(p117)*.

↑ Listening to a trumpet solo in cozy club Fritzel's

Let's Dance

Folk-heavy stylings of Cajun and Zydeco (p189) are played around the city, with groups like the Lost Bayou Ramblers packing out venues. It's hard not to join in the dancing, so brush up on your two- and three-step, and away you go! Tipitina's hosts a Zydeco night on alternate Sundays (tipitinas.com), or for a Cajun dance party, make for Mulates (www.mulates. com). Meanwhile for jazzy swing dance lessons, both the Spotted Cat (p117) and AllWays Lounge (p45) host low-key swing nights, on Wednesdays and Sundays respectively.

←

Taking a swing dance lesson at Frenchmen Street institution, the Spotted Cat

TOP 4 NEW ORLEANS MUSICIANS

Trombone Shorty
Taking the sounds of brass bands into the modern scene with exciting collaborations.

Irma Thomas
The Soul Queen of New Orleans, in the style of Aretha Franklin and Etta James.

Big Freedia
At the vanguard of the "bounce" scene and beloved by Beyoncé.

Tank and the Bangas
A female-fronted band that blends styles to lead the future of New Orleans' music.

Bold As Brass

So many children grow up playing in brass bands here that it's no wonder the hubbub of trumpets, saxophones, and trombones is the all-pervading soundtrack to the city. Wander the streets and you'll likely catch Second Lines parading downtown neighborhoods (p114), and brass bands playing swing jazz on the corner of Frenchmen Street. There are countless local legends worth a listen, from traditional ensembles to the hip-hop and funk stylings of the Hot 8 Brass Band and Dirty Dozen Brass Band. Make for the Maple Leaf Bar on Tuesdays to catch grammy-winning brass stars Rebirth (www. mapleleafbar.com). On Wednesdays, hole up in cozy neighborhood Candlelight Lounge to see the Treme Brass Band play (925 North Robertson Street).

→

Musicians performing on the street in the heart of the French Quarter

The French Connection

The French colony of La Nouvelle -Orléans was founded in 1718, and traces of France still abound today. French words and phrases pepper the city's language and place names: the French Quarter is known as the Vieux Carré ("old square"). Tour the quarter with Friends of the Cabildo (p69) and you'll pass Napoleon house, intended as a residence for the emperor in exile (p81), and the Ursuline Convent, built in 1734 - the Mississippi Valley's oldest building(p92). And you can't miss St. Louis Cathedral, proclaiming the faith of the first catholic French settlers (p62).

↑ The 18th-century Napoleon House, now a restaurant

NEW ORLEANS FOR
HISTORY BUFFS

For more than 300 years, French, Spanish, African, and Cajun cultures have given rise to New Orleans some of America's most colorful history. Numerous reminders of these influences remain, from old churches and crumbling cemeteries, to historic houses and a host of specialist museums.

 TOP 3
MUSEUMS OF NEW ORLEANS HISTORY

Historic New Orleans Collection
Delve deep into the city's history at this museum with its extensive array of maps and artifacts (p72).

Presbytère
Exhibits focus on Mardi Gras and Hurricane Katrina in this former colonial courthouse on Jackson Square (p64).

The Whitney Plantation
Guided tours and detailed exhibits at this former River Road plantation house (p184) explore Louisiana's plantation history.

20th Century

During World War II, New Orleans' shipyards built thousands of the boats used by Allied troups: explore this legacy at the National World War II Museum (p126). In 2005, Hurricane Katrina swept through the city (p54). Pay homage to those who lost their lives in the disaster with a visit to Mid-City's memorial in St. Patrick's Cemetery #1 (p162), and in the Warehouse District (p120), see the striking Scrap House sculpture in Mississippi River Heritage Park.

African American Heritage

The city owes much of its unique cultural heritage to the enslaved African peoples brought here in colonial times. This legacy is preserved in Congo Square (p108), where festivals like Jazz Fest (p172) celebrate African American culture. Make sure to visit the Backstreet Cultural Museum to learn about the carnival traditions of Mardi Gras Indians (p115). Beyond the city, the Whitney explores the history of Louisiana plantations from the perspective of those enslaved (p184).

↑ Musicians performing in Congo Square during Jazz Fest

Streets of History

Stroll into the past in New Orleans' historic neighborhoods (p100). In Faubourg Marigny and Bywater (p104), admire colorful Creole cottages and shotgun houses, home to French Creoles, German immigrants, and African Americans from the early 19th century. In the Garden District (p138), eclectic mansions hold stories of the wealthy bankers, planters, and merchants who lived here.

← Colorful shotgun house in Bywater

Signs of Spain

New Orleans was colonized by Spain from 1763 until 1803 and there are still traces of the country in the brightly painted buildings and ornate ironwork galleries in the French Quarter. Look out for the special tiled street signs hinting at the city's Iberian influence - Calle de Borbon for Bourbon Street , Calle Real for Royal Street, and Calle de San Luis for St Louis Street. The Spanish spirit is kept alive with the Running of the Bull, now enacted without live animals, and Mardi Gras - festivals that both originated under Spanish rule.

→ Celebrating the Running of the Bull festival

↑ The Hurricane Katrina Memorial, St. Patrick's Cemetery

Spiritual Homes

The Sazerac is a New Orleanian whiskey cocktail that dates back to the mid-19th century, and there's no finer place to drink one than at its namesake bar at the Roosevelt Hotel *(p133)*. This is also the birthplace of the Ramos Gin Fizz, an effervescent citrusy creation. The Grasshopper was invented by Tujague's bartenders in 1918, and you can still enjoy this minty tipple at the iconic spot *(tujaguesrestaurant.com)*.

←

Sazeracs served straight up, without ice, at the Roosevelt Hotel

NEW ORLEANS
COCKTAIL
HOUR

A long tradition of good drinking is one of New Orleans' trademarks, so it's no surprise that the Sazerac, Ramos Gin Fizz, and the Grasshopper were all invented here. Concoct your own cocktail tour, toast a host of historic venues, and explore the unique mixology of the Crescent City.

Get Schooled

Cocktail connoisseurs and aspiring masters of mixology can dive into the history of the South's cocktail culture at the Museum of the American Cocktail, part of the Southern Food and Beverage Museum *(p148)*. Along with antique items of bar kit, the museum showcases cultural influences of the cocktail with regular seminars. To really get into the spirit of things, catch the Tales of the Cocktail Festival, a week-long event that takes over the city's bars with special mixing lessons and tastings *(talesofthecocktail.org)*.

→

Cocktail bar party and tastings during Tales of the Cocktail Festival

Drink Up

Cocktails always taste better with a view, so head up to the city's cool rooftop bars for fresher air and a scenic skyline. Downtown, the CBD is the place to be, with hotel bars often the swankiest option. Monkey Board at the Troubadour Hotel has a relaxed vibe and a casual kitchen (monkeyboardnola. com), while the rooftop bar at the Catahoula Hotel serves pisco-flavored beverages, Peruvian nibbles, and lovely vistas (catahoulahotel.com). In the Garden District, head up to the Pontchartrain Hotel's rooftop spot, Hot Tin, for scenic sundowners overlooking the Mississippi River (hottinbar.com).

→

Enjoying a drink with friends at the Catahoula Hotel's rooftop terrace

← A bartender serving an icy absinthe-based cocktail

TOP 5 LOCAL COCKTAILS

Sazerac
Rye whiskey, absinthe, and Peychaud bitters combine in this classic.

Ramos Gin Fizz
Two separate shaking processes create a fluffy, sweet-tasting breakfast delight.

Grasshopper
Crème de menthe lends this after-dinner favorite its bright green color and minty flavor.

Brandy Milk Punch
Vanilla, nutmeg, brandy, and cream combine in this brunch-time cocktail.

Hurricane
The signature sweet rum cocktail at French Quarter stalwart, Pat O'Brien's.

Swamp Thing

New Orleans is surrounded by soupy swamps and bayous, best investigated on a boat tour. Head for Honey Island Swamp and glide through the back-waters in a flatbottomed boat with Cajun Encounters *(cajunencounters. com)*. Drift along channels lined with gnarly cypress trees, and look out for wildlife like turtles, pelicans, snakes, and alligators. If you prefer to stay on dry land, head to Barataria Preserve, and soak up the reserve's mysterious beauty as you wander the network of boardwalk trails *(p194)*.

↑ Swamp alligator relaxing on a log

NEW ORLEANS FOR
THE GREAT OUTDOORS

Though it's best known for its historic urban quarters, New Orleans has plenty of broad green parks and leafy streets where you can beat the heat and escape the city buzz. And the mighty Mississippi offers more outdoor pursuits, from riverside strolls to exciting swamp tours.

Paddling along Bayou St. John as dusk descends ↑

Let It Roll

With over 100 miles (161 km) of designated bike trails and flat streets laid out on a grid plan, New Orleans is a bike friendly city. Cycle scheme Blue Bike has dozens of stations across the city, and Wheelin' Bikes offers guided tours (p207). Hitch a ride and pedal the French Quarter, roll along the riverfront, or wheel to City Park along the Lafitte Greenway.

→

Wheeling through the city on Blue Bikes

Cool Off in the Park

City Park makes a refreshing escape from the heat, with its paths shaded by Spanish moss and the largest grove of mature live oaks in the world, and lagoons to explore by paddle boat (p176). Audubon Park is another great green space, with a golf course and recreation areas (p156). In Bywater, Crescent Park runs along the river, offering meandering bike trails and waterside picnic spots (p119).

←

Fountains and bright tropical borders in Audubon Park

A City On the Water

Whether you're gliding through the waters on a gleaming paddlewheeler or strolling a riverfront path, the mighty Mississippi is a thrill. The Steamboat *Natchez* has plied these waters for nearly 100 years, and a river cruise on this old steamer is a must (p74). In Mid-City, Bayou St. John is a peaceful spot for kayaking or a picnic along the banks (p173). Anglers can cast their lines into the vast Lake Pontchartrain at the city's northern end, and there are charter fishing tours into the coastal waterways with Salty Dog Charters (saltydog chartersllc.com) or the Redfish Charter Company (redfishcharterco.com).

> HIDDEN GEM
> ### Picnic on the Fly
>
> At the southernmost riverfront end of Audubon Park (p156), Butterfly Riverview Park is a great chill-out spot. Locals call it "the Fly" and come here to soak up the sun, for picnics and parties, or to watch the sun set over the Mississippi.

World-Class Museums

Fine-art connoisseurs won't be disappointed here, with a host of grand museums to explore. The New Orleans Museum of Art (NOMA) holds a vast collection of international masterpieces *(p166)*, and beside it, the Besthoff Sculpture Garden makes for dreamy strolling in the open air *(p167)*. Housed in a futuristic glass and steel building, the Ogden Museum of Southern Art's wide-ranging collections cover works by Louisiana artists *(p134)*. Across the street, at the New Orleans Contemporary Arts Center, you'll find everything from paintings to installations and performance art *(p134)*.

NEW ORLEANS FOR
ART LOVERS

With its sultry setting, laid-back atmosphere, and vibrant history, it's easy to see why this city has long been a haven for artists. New Orleans makes for an ever-changing canvas of world-class fine art, colorful street murals, and whimsical folk art creations.

Striking Street Art

Adding to the city's eclectic art scene are a host of striking and thought-provoking street murals. The best places to see these are in Marigny and Bywater, where colorful works adorn the walls of second-hand shops and trendy cafés *(p104)*. Wander St. Claude Avenue, sometimes called the "Mural Mile," to spot several colorful works, including a huge painting, *Third Lines*, by Henry Lipkis which depicts the city's Second Line parades. Head to Studio Be warehouse which showcases the work of celebrated New Orleans artist and activist Brandon Odums *(p118)*.

Cycling past jazz funeral-inspired street art in Bywater

HIDDEN GEM
Algiers Folk Art
Take the ferry to Algiers
(p128) to visit the Folk
Art Zone and Blues
Museum (appointment
only), where the self-
taught artist Charles
Gillam's colorful works
explore Louisiana's
rich musical heritage
(folkartzone.org).

← *Stormy* (2015) by
local artist MaPo
Kinnord, exhibited
at NOMA

Local Treasures

This creative city has an impressive line-up
of venues exhibiting home-grown talent. In
the heart of the Warehouse (or Arts) District,
Le Mieux Galleries champions emerging and
established names *(www.lemieuxgalleries.
com)*. In the French Quarter, George Rodrigue
Studio exhibits distinctive Blue Dog paintings
by the late Cajun artist *(georgerodrigue.com)*,
and in the CBD the Stella Jones Gallery, showcases modern African
American artists
*(www.stellajones
gallery.com)*.

David Lambert's *Corner
Bar* at Les Mieux Galleries

Be Part of the Art

Unsurprisingly, this party city
holds arts festivals through the
year. Two of the biggest are the
Arts District's Hancock Whitney
White Linen Night *(www.
cacwhitelinennight.com)* and
Art for Art's Sake, on Magazine
Street. Both are joyful street
parties with gallery openings,
music, food, and more. Outside
festival season, you can watch
highly skilled artists blowing
glass during free daily demonstrations at the New Orleans
Glassworks and Printmaking
Studio, and even blow your own
glass during mini-workshops
(neworleansglassworks.com).

→
Glass blowing workshop
at New Orleans Glassworks
and Printmaking Studio

Wander the Markets

Make for the famous French Market to shop for souvenirs in the city's most historic retail setting *(p90)*. At the adjoining French Quarter Flea Market, you'll find vendors selling everything from wood carvings to colorful woven bags. Meanwhile the nightly bazaar at Palace Market Frenchmen is held in a lively outdoor lot amid clubs and bars – this is city's best spot for sourcing unique local works of art *(p117)*.

←

Shoppers browsing the French Quarter Flea Market

NEW ORLEANS FOR
SHOPPERS

Whether it's hunting for outlet mall bargains, wandering bustling markets, or browsing unique boutiques for art, music, and fashion, New Orleans offers plenty for keen shoppers. This city is so full of irresistible treasures, you might want to bring an extra suitcase.

Meander Through Malls

Stretching out alongside the Mississippi, the Outlet Collection at Riverwalk is the country's first downtown outlet center *(p129)*. Browse this huge department store for bargains, from leather handbags to Levi's and other classic American brands. For upscale shopping, Canal Place *(p130)* houses designer fashion at Saks Fifth Avenue and Michael Kors, and jewelry at Tiffany & Co. In the French Quarter, Jax Brewery on Decatur Street is set in a former beer factory – today it makes a pleasant spot to seek out clothing and souvenirs with a New Orleans flair.

→

The city's most upmarket shopping mall, Canal Place, also home to a hotel and cinema

Magazine Street

For leisurely shopping, take a stroll along Magazine Street. This 6-mile (9.7-km) stretch of the Garden District *(p138)* features clothing and home decor boutiques, antique dealers and independent bookstores, delightful eateries, and historic homes. Browse vintage fashion at Funky Monkey *(funky monkeynola.com)* or peruse gilded treasures at Antiques on Jackson *(antiquesonjackson.com)*.

Wandering Magazine Street, and *(inset)* hunting for antique jewellery ↑

SHOPS

Louisiana Music Factory

Renowned indie record store specializing in local music.

🏠 421 Frenchmen Street 🌐 louisiana musicfactory.com

Maskerade

A store where you can buy artisanal Mardi Gras masks all year round.

🏠 620 St Ann Street 🌐 themaskstore.com

Rouse's Market

French Quarter grocery selling beignet mix and NOLA foodstuffs.

🏠 701 Royal Street 🌐 rouses.com

↑ An antique lamp store in New Orleans' French Quarter

Quest for Antiques

Since its earliest days, New Orleans has always been a treasure trove of rare and remarkable collectibles. The city is studded with antique dealers, with some of the finest to be found on Royal Street *(p70)*: Keil's glitters with crystal chandeliers and French enamel jewellery *(p71)*, while M.S. Rau brims with elaborate silverware and objets d'art *(p71)*. Beyond the French Quarter, Magazine Street Antique Mall is a horde of heirlooms and vintage pieces *(www.magazinestreet.com)*.

Water-based
fun at Cool Zoo in
Audubon Zoo ↑

NEW ORLEANS FOR
FAMILIES

With a multitude of open-air and indoor attractions on offer, New Orleans
is a superb city to explore if you're visiting with children. From hands-on
museums and carnival exhibits, to expansive green spaces and lush
nature preserves, the Crescent City has something for kids of all ages.

Park the Kids

This city is peppered with
green spaces, and spots like
Audubon Park *(p156)* and vast
City Park *(p170)* are perfect
for when kids need to let off
steam. In City Park's fairytale playground, Storyland,
little ones can clamber aboard
Captain Hook's ship or climb
inside Cinderella's pumpkin
carriage, or take a spin on an
antique merry-go-round in
the Carousel Gardens. Meanwhile riverside Crescent Park
offers grassy stretches for
picnicking, and meandering
bike paths to cycle *(p119)*.

→

A tree-lined avenue in
verdant Audubon Park

Explore the Natural World

Aspiring naturalists will delight in citywide attractions of the world-renowned Audubon Nature Institute. Creatures from around the globe roam their natural habitats at the Audubon Zoo (p144), while the underwater worlds of mesmerizing jellyfish, rare seahorses, and playful otters are on display at the vast Audubon Aquarium of the Americas (p124). The Audubon Butterfly Garden and Insectarium (p131) keeps bug hunters busy with its creepy crawly exhibits – look out for an interactive cooking show where visitors are invited to taste edible bugs. Outside the city, intrepid explorers should board a boat tour of Barataria Preserve's steamy green swampland (p194) – just make sure to watch out for the 'gators!

← Admiring entrancing displays at the Audubon Aquarium of the Americas

EAT

Reginelli's Pizzeria
Kids can create their own pizza at this casual eatery, while adults enjoy the range of delicious toppings, salads, and wines by the glass.

⌂ 3244 Magazine Street
Ⓦ reginellis.com

Ⓢ Ⓢ Ⓢ

Muriels
A great children's menu and crayons keep the kids content at this fine-dining restaurant in the French Quarter.

⌂ 801 Chartres Street
Ⓦ muriels.com

Ⓢ Ⓢ Ⓢ

Rainy-Day Favorites

If the sun doesn't shine (or indeed if it's too hot outside) there's still plenty to entertain young minds. Get stuck into hands-on exhibits and games at the Louisiana Children's Museum (p170) or head to the New Orleans Museum of Art (p166), which keeps kids entertained with story time, art workshops, and child-focused tours. Another good indoor option is Mardi Gras World (p149), where you can wander among giant characters in a warehouse of carnival floats and dress up in krewe costumes.

→ Throwing goodies from a float at Mardi Gras World

🔍 HIDDEN GEM
On Track

In a quiet corner of the New Orleans Botanical Garden (p171), the Historic Train Garden features mini replicas of the city's trains and streetcars. On weekends the carriages run through a model of the city (10:30am – 4:30pm).

Literary Events

The city's best-known literary happening is the Tennessee Williams/New Orleans Literary Festival, held around the playwright's birthday on March 26 *(ten nesseewilliams.net)*. The five-day event features talks by authors, workshops, and writing contests. Also in March, the Saints and Sinners Literary Festival focuses on works by LGBT+ authors *(sas fest.org)*. November sees the Words and Music Festival laid on by the Faulkner Society *(wordsandmusic.org)*.

Literary talk at the Tennessee Williams/New Orleans Festival

NEW ORLEANS FOR
BOOKWORMS

With its lush setting, eccentric cast of characters, and fascinating history, it's no surprise that New Orleans has inspired an impressive list of writers. Their legacy can be found in a trail of literary landmarks, book stores, festivals, and a wealth of prize-winning novels that bring the city to life.

Resident Writers

From William Faulkner to Tennessee Williams, New Orleans has been home to many world-famous authors and playwrights. Wander through the characterful French Quarter, and you'll pass 711 Royal Street, where NOLA-native Truman Capote wrote his first novel *Other Voices, Other Rooms*; and 722 Toulouse St where playwright Tennessee Williams drafted his famous drama *A Streetcar Named Desire*. Today, these buildings form part of the Historic New Orleans Collection *(p72)*, which explores the lives of Capote and Williams in its exhibits. Make sure to visit elegant Beauregard-Keyes House *(p93)* to pay homage to Frances Parkinson Keyes, who penned many of her novels here during the 1950s, and pick up a good read at Faulkner House Books *(p79)* – William Faulkner lived at this address while writing his first novel, *Soldier's Pay*.

Truman Capote, one of the city's numerous literary luminaries

Falkner House Books, one-time home of William Faulkner

Follow the Plot

New Orleans is peppered with sights immortalized in works of fiction. Trace the plot of Tennessee Williams' *A Streetcar Named Desire* and grab a bite at traditional French-Creole haunt Galatoire's *(p77)* – this is where Blanche and Stella DuBois dine at the start of the play. Or, catch a ride on the St. Charles Streetcar *(p142)*, which inspired the play's title. At 819 Canal Street a bronze statue depicts Ignatius J. Reilly, the main character in John Kennedy Toole's *A Confederacy of Dunces*. Fans of Anne Rice's *Interview with a Vampire* should take a tour around St. Louis Cemetery #1 *(p112)*.

New Orleans' famous St. Charles Avenue Streetcar, trundling along as it has done for more than 150 years

---

TOP 5 — BOOKS SET IN NEW ORLEANS

Dinner at Antoine's (1948)
Frances Parkinson Keyes romance set in 1940s New Orleans.

Interview with a Vampire (1976)
The first in the *Vampire Chronicles* series by Anne Rice.

A Confederacy of Dunces (1980)
Published after the author John Kennedy Toole's suicide, won the Pulitzer Prize for Fiction.

Why New Orleans Matters (2005)
A post-Katrina memoir by Tom Piazza.

What Went Missing and What Got Found (2015)
Evocative contemporary short stories from Fatima Shaik.

Bourbon Street

This legendary street never sleeps. Spend a night dipping in and out of the bars and restaurants lining the strip, or linger in one of the famous jazz bars (p77). This is the heartland of the "go-cup" (most places will serve your drink in a plastic cup to go) – so you can wander along, cocktail in hand, and soak up the party atmosphere.

> **INSIDER TIP**
> **Late Night Haunts**
>
> For night-time chills, follow French Quarter Phantoms on a walking tour of the Vieux Carré. Their Ghost and Vampire trail leads you through the quarter's spookiest spots (frenchquarter phantoms.com).

↑ Neon-lit Bourbon Street thronging with revellers

NEW ORLEANS FOR
NIGHTLIFE

Mardi Gras might be this party city's biggest shindig, but there are *bons temps* to be had here all year round. With late-night shows and comedy gigs, burlesque and drag shows, 24-hour diners, and even night-time ghost tours, you're sure to have a good time after dark.

Laughing Matters

Comedy-lovers are sure to get their funny fix here, with the city's lively stand-up scene and big-name shows to enjoy. Without a dedicated comedy club, open-mic nights take place in bars around the city, and almost all are free. Head to St. Claude for a clutch of venues with comic credentials: AllWays Lounge, Siberia Lounge (siberialounge.com), and the HiHo Lounge (hiho lounge.net). For famous comics and standout shows, make for the Saenger (p133) and Joy theaters (thejoytheater.com).

↑ Stand up comedian performing at Hiho Lounge in St. Claude

24-Hour Patty People

If you're in need of a midnight feast or an early-hours burger, there are plenty of options in this 24/7 city. Make Port of Call your first stop - this late night dive delivers juicy burgers and a jukebox *(port ofcallnola.com)*. Meanwhile local favorite Clover Grill serves its burgers cooked under a Cadillac wheel cap *(www.clovergrill.com)*, and neighborhood joint Buffa's is known for its late plates and live music *(buffasrestaurant. com)*. If you're craving something sweet, there's no line at the typically teeming Café du Monde at 3 am *(p96)*.

←

Enjoying late-night beignets at 24-hour Café du Monde

Venerable Venues

The city's grandest venues have been revitalized and refurbished since the damage sustained during Hurricane Katrina. The luxurious Saenger *(p133)* and neighboring Joy both host broadway productions, live music, and comedy shows. Across Canal Street, the Orpheum has impeccable accoustics, and often hosts the Louisiana Philharmonic Orchestra *(orpheumnola.com)*.

→

Watching a concert at the Saenger Theatre

High Tease

Cabaret's proud history stretches back to the golden era of Bourbon Street, but these days, the best burlesque, drag, and cabaret shows can be found elsewhere too. St. Claude's charmingly louche AllWays Lounge and Theater holds sequin-spangled drag nights, and outlandish peep shows *(theallwayslounge.net)*. Meanwhile in the heart of the French Quarter, One Eyed Jacks is known for its weird and wonderful Fleur de Tease show *(oneeyedjacks.net)*.

←

Cabaret show at the AllWays Lounge and Theater

A YEAR IN
NEW ORLEANS

JANUARY

Twelfth Night *(5 Jan.)* Joyous parades mark the official start of Carnival season and the build-up to Mardi Gras.

△ **King Cake Festival** *(late Jan.)* Local bakeries compete in Champions Square to win the title of best King Cake in the city.

FEBRUARY

△ **Mardi Gras** *(Feb., sometimes early Mar.)* After a month of celebrating, the city gears up for Lundi Gras and Fat Tuesday with more parties.

Tet Fest *(Feb.)* Vietnamese New Year is honored with traditional music, food, and dancing at Mary Queen of Vietnamese church.

MAY

Treme/7th Ward Arts and Culture Fest *(early May)* Food, activities, and music in this historic African American neighborhood.

△ **Bayou Boogaloo** *(mid May)* A free, one-day music festival celebrates a mix of local bands on the bayou waterfront in Mid City.

JUNE

Pride *(early Jun.)* A huge weekend for the LGBT+ community, with a downtown Saturday evening parade and parties across various venues.

△ **Creole Tomato Festival** *(early Jun.)* The French Market is filled with local vendors selling everything from Bloody Marys to tomato ice cream.

Cajun Zydeco Fest *(late Jun.)* Louis Armstrong Park hosts a huge line up of Cajun music and Zydeco.

SEPTEMBER

△ **Football Season** *(early Sep.)* Sundays become football days as the New Orleans Saints begin their regular season games at the Superdome.

NOLA on Tap *(mid-Sep.)* The Gulf Coast's largest beer festival takes over the Festival Grounds in City Park, with over 400 different beers on offer.

OCTOBER

Halloween *(late Oct.)* The city dresses up and parades – see some of the best costumes as people wander up and down Frenchmen.

△ **Voodoo Fest** *(late Oct.)* A weekend music festival in City Park attracting international acts from the worlds of rock and pop.

MARCH

△ **The Tennessee Williams Festival** *(Mar.)*
The region's biggest literary event takes over the
Monteleone Hotel and other city venues with
panels, readings, and theatrical productions.
St. Patrick's Day *(mid Mar.)* Various events take
place as the city's American-Irish population
celebrate with Mardi Gras-style parades.

APRIL

New Orleans Wine and Food Experience *(early
Apr.)* A festival celebrating the city's food scene
with a huge tasting in the Superdome and a
culinary stroll down Royal Street.
△ **French Quarter Fest** *(Apr.)* A free festival in
the French Quarter with a diverse mix of music
and local food vendors across three days.
Jazz Fest *(late Apr.)* The city's biggest music
festival stretches over two weekends, with jazz,
blues, rock, and pop music, and tasty food too.

JULY

Essence Festival *(early Jul.)* A huge festival
held at the Superdome and around the city
featuring soul, RnB, and hip-hop artists.
Running of the Bulls *(12th Jul.)* New Orleans'
version of Spain's famous San Fermín event,
with roller-derby girls taking the place of
bulls, and chasing participants through town.
△ **Tales of the Cocktail** *(mid-late Jul.)*
The world's alcohol brands host demonstrations and special events at all the major
cocktail and hotel bars.

AUGUST

Satchmo SummerFest *(early Aug.)* A weekend of
jazz and brass honouring Louis Armstrong.
△ **Southern Decadence** *(late Aug.)* A brash
and raunchy six-day celebration of LGBT+ culture
culminates on Labor Day.
Museum Month *(throughout Aug.)* Participating
museums offer free entry to all visitors.

NOVEMBER

△ **PoBoy Fest** *(mid Nov.)* Sandwich makers
vie for prizes in a hotly contested festival of
the city's favorite dish.
Treme Creole Gumbo Fest *(mid Nov.)* Louis
Armstrong Park welcomes brass bands and
gumbo variations from the city's restaurants.
Bayou Classic *(Thanksgiving Weekend)*
Football fixture between Grambling and
Southern University at the Superdome.

DECEMBER

△ **Celebration in the Oaks** *(Dec.)* City Park
transforms with dozens of light installations,
food stalls, and music tents.
Lune Fete *(mid Dec.)* Local light artists set up
innovative light installations around the CBD.
New Year's Eve *(31st Dec.)* Fireworks on the
Mississippi River, best viewed from the banks
near the French Quarter, mark the start of the
New Year.

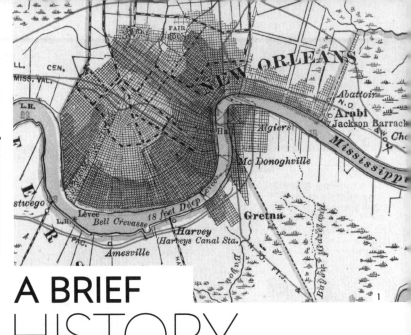

A BRIEF
HISTORY

One of the U.S.'s oldest cities, New Orleans has survived wars, epidemics, and natural disasters. With a rich musical heritage and distinctive traditions, the city continues to forge its own unique identity from the cultures of the many peoples that have shaped it.

Arrival of the French

Long before Europeans arrived in the early 18th century, Louisiana was populated by American Indian peoples, including the Chitimacha and Taensa tribes, who thrived in towns on the shores of Lake Pontchartrain. When the Spanish and then the French arrived in Louisiana they encroached on traditional hunting grounds, introducing diseases that decimated indigenous populations. In 1718, Jean-Baptiste Le Moyne, Sieur de Bienville, established Nouvelle-Orléans on the Lower Mississippi. Amid flooding swampland and a pestilent climate, the early colony did not prosper. Whenever immigration to the new colony

1720

La Nouvelle-Orléans is declared the capital of French Louisiana.

Timeline of events

1682
French explorer La Salle reaches the Mississippi, claiming Louisiana for Louis XIV.

1718
Jean Baptiste Le Moyne, Sieur de Bienville, establishes a French settlement.

1720
The first ship of enslaved people is brought to New Orleans on July 7.

c. 10,000 BC
Louisiana is populated by the first Paleo-Indian peoples.

1763
Treaty of Paris signed; Louisiana and New Orleans ceded to Spain.

diminished, prisoners and prostitutes were deported from France to replenish the population. Meanwhile brutal treatment by European settlers incited unrest among indigenous populations, with the Natchez revolt rising in 1729, and the Chickasaw Wars fought from the early 1720s into the 1760s.

Spanish City

From 1755, the Seven Years' War saw Britain, France, and Spain struggle for control of North America. Before signing the Treaty of Paris, which ended the war in 1763, Louis XV secretly ceded Louisiana to his cousin, the Spanish King Charles III. From 1763 into the 1790s the city was propelled to prosperity as trade with the Americans increased. In 1796 Jean Étienne de Boré first granulated sugar on a commercial scale, ushering in the age of sugar production in Louisiana. Plantations were established, relying on the labor of thousands of enslaved Africans. From 1804, New Orleans received an infusion of Creole refugees who had fled the 1791 Revolution in French colony Saint Domingue (now Haiti). Doubling the city's population, they added a distinct Caribbean flavor to the colony, building West Indian-style houses, and expanding the practice of voodoo in the colony.

1 A map of New Orleans from the early 1900s.

2 French explorer La Salle is received in the Mississippi delta by the Taensa peoples, before claiming the territory for France in 1682.

3 Bienville lays out plans for the city of La Nouvelle-Orléans, 1718.

4 Pitot House, an example of the West-Indian-style plantation houses brought to the city by Haitian refugees.

1775–83
Revolutionary War wages, as American states fight for independence from Britain.

1795
United States and Spain sign a treaty opening the Mississippi River to American trade.

1765
First Acadians arrive from Nova Scotia, settling west of New Orleans.

1788
Fire on March 21 (Good Friday) destroys 856 buildings in the French Quarter.

1791
Toussaint L'Ouverture leads revolt in Saint Domingue (Haiti).

The Louisiana Purchase and the Battle of New Orleans

Spain ceded Louisiana to France in 1800, but Napoleon soon sold the land to the United States for $15 million to help fund his wars in Europe. On December 20, 1803, under President Jefferson, the Louisiana Purchase was officially ratified. Along with territories stretching to the Rocky Mountains, Louisiana was signed away by the French, and the U.S. almost doubled in size. Following the transfer, Louisiana was admitted to the Union on April 30, 1812, six weeks before the United States declared war on Great Britain. In January 1815, despite the Treaty of Ghent, which had ended the war the month before, British forces launched a fresh attack on New Orleans. General Andrew Jackson led an army of pirates, frontiersmen, gentlemen, and free men of color in the Battle of New Orleans, beating back the British and bringing an end to the hostilities of the War of 1812.

Steamboats, Cotton, and Sugar

In the early 19th century, the cotton industry flourished in the South thanks to advances in technology such as the invention

1 Cheering the 1803 Louisiana Purchase.

2 Battle of New Orleans in 1815.

3 Port of New Orleans.

4 Nuns tend victims of a yellow fever epidemic.

324

million dollars in trade was cleared by New Orleans' steamboats in 1860.

Timeline of events

1800
Louisiana ceded from Spain back to France.

1803
Louisiana Purchase ratified on December 20, the state is sold to the U.S.

1812
The first steamboat, the *New Orleans*, arrives in the city in January.

1812
Louisiana admitted to the Union on April 30.

1814
Treaty of Ghent, signed on December 24, ends the War of 1812.

of the cotton gin and development of the steamboat. With its favorable position on the Mississippi, New Orleans became a significant port from which cotton was shipped to the rest of the world. A thriving domestic slave trade sustained labor on the city's plantations, where cash crops of cotton, tobacco, indigo, and sugarcane were cultivated by enslaved people, often under brutal conditions.

With increasing global exports of commodities, the city's economy boomed. By 1845, it was the second most significant port in the nation after New York, and the largest city in the South, with a population of 168,000. Immense wealth led to expansion; in 1852 the French Opera House was built and the city developed its reputation for courtly life, gambling, and easy living. Europeans continued to arrive, with many Germans settling upstream from New Orleans as farmers, and Irish people east of Louisiana Avenue. Between 1817 and 1860 the city was blighted by epidemics of cholera and yellow fever, with 23 epidemics killing more than 28,000. Meanwhile, bitter tensions over the issue of slavery fomented between the South and the North, where laws had freed many of those in bondage by the end of the 18th century.

↑ Docker loading a cotton bale onto a steamboat

1815

Andrew Jackson leads the Battle of New Orleans, defeating the British on January 8.

1820–1830

Development of the city's steamboats opens trade to the interior of the country.

1831–5

New Orleans becomes the world's largest cotton market.

1852

The city of Lafayette is annexed, becoming the Garden District.

1853

Yellow fever epidemic kills 8,000 between July and November.

Civil War and Reconstruction

The Civil War brought an end to the city's prosperity. In 1861, Louisiana seceded from the Union and in 1862, New Orleans was captured and subject to harsh military occupation. After the war, the city struggled to recover – its plantatations, the source of its wealth, were destroyed. Enslaved people were freed in 1865, but lived in legal limbo. Federal troops withdrew in 1877, but legal and social gains made by African Americans during Reconstruction were eroded as Confederates resumed power. The 1884 Cotton Centennial Exposition was launched in a bid to stimulate the languishing economy, but far fewer visitors attended than expected, and the city lost millions of dollars.

20th-Century New Orleans

In the early 20th century, the city emerged as the birthplace of jazz, with the new improvisational style of music flourishing in the bars of Storyville *(p116)*. Though World War I briefly boosted business in the shipyards, New Orleans suffered greatly during the Depression of the early 1930s. In World War II, business returned to the shipyards, the site of production for boats used

↑ Carpenter working on a World War II boat at a New Orleans shipyard

Timeline of events

1861–5
Civil War between the Union (North) and the Confederates (South).

1896
Supreme Court decision Plessy v. Ferguson permits racial segregation.

1917
Storyville deemed too tempting for World War I sailors, and abolished on October 2.

1862
Union General Benjamin "Beast" Butler occupies the city on May 1.

1877
Reconstruction ends; federal troops leave New Orleans.

in Allied landings. Under the mayoralty of deLesseps Story Morrison (1946–1961), the city experienced a period of regeneration, with the construction of the Pontchartrain Expressway and Crescent City Connection. This era saw progress in civil rights too: desegregation of public education began in 1954, and the Voting Rights Act of 1965 changed the political landscape. In 1978, Ernest N. "Dutch" Morial was elected as the city's first African American mayor. Following the Fall of Saigon in 1975, Vietnamese refugees began to settle in New Orleans, adding to the rich diversity of the city.

New Orleans Today

In the wake of Hurricane Katrina, New Orleans is steadily recovering, with restoration works ongoing (p54). In 2011, the Mississippi reached historic flood stages, but the levees held. In 2017, the City Council removed four controversial confederate monuments, declaring the statues a public nuisance. For the city's 2018 Tricentennial celebrations, grand new parks and facilities were established, allowing New Orleanian food, music, and art scenes to shine like never before.

1 During the Civil War, Federal troops occupy the city in 1862, under Union General Benjamin "Beast" Butler.

2 Attendees from around the globe arrive at the city's 1884 Cotton Centennial Exposition.

3 The huge cantilever bridge, the Crescent City Connection, links the city's north and south across the Mississippi.

4 Musical performance honoring New Orlean's 2018 Tricentennial.

1975
The Louisiana Superdome constructed, at a cost of $163 million.

1954
Supreme Court ruling Brown v. the Board of Education orders the desegregation of public schools.

2010
The BP oil spill seeps into the Gulf of Mexico and Lake Pontchartrain.

2005
Hurricane Katrina hits on August 29. Floodwaters inundate 80 percent of the city.

2018
Latoya Cantrell is sworn in as the first female mayor of New Orleans.

HURRICANE KATRINA

Hitting New Orleans in August 2005, Hurricane Katrina has been called the most devastating disaster in U.S. history. More than 850,000 homes were damaged, and entire communities were destroyed overnight. The official death toll in Louisiana alone exceeded 1,800 people, and millions more were left homeless. The recovery effort has been a monumental undertaking: billions of dollars in insurance proceeds and government funds have been committed so far.

IMPACT OF THE HURRICANE

Katrina was a disaster of unprecedented magnitude, combining the destructive force of a powerful hurricane, a huge storm surge of seawater, and levee failures that left much of the city inundated by floodwaters for weeks. In the wake of the disaster, the city descended into chaos, with desperate citizens left pleading for help from their rooftops or sheltering in the Superdome in appalling conditions. The Federal Emergency Management Agency (FEMA) was criticized for its slow and fitful response, but eventually the military arrived to oversee a massive evacuation. The flooded city sat virtually empty as residents spread out across the US in search of shelter. Beginning in late 2005, residents slowly started returning to the city.

A NEW NEW ORLEANS

New Orleans' resilient spirit and improvisation have fueled the city's recovery. Today, it is possible to visit the city without seeing a trace of the disaster, but outside the historic areas, signs of the devastation still linger. Though the population remains significantly smaller than before the disaster, many residents have returned. Recovery continues on a block-by-block basis and the Army Corps of Engineers are building and maintaining a more advanced flood control system to protect the city.

WHY THE LEVEES FAILED

New Orleans relies on a network of man-made canals and earthen levees to drain water from the low-lying city into Lake Pontchartrain. The storm surge from Hurricane Katrina forced a massive amount of water from the lake back into the canals. Water cascaded over the canal walls with such force that their earthen supports collapsed and floodwater poured into the city.

Aug. 28, 2005

Mayor Ray Nagin orders the mandatory evacuation of the city: thousands leave, but many others stay put.

Sep. 15, 2005

President Bush pledges to rebuild the city.

Aug. 26, 2005

△ Storm-track forecasts zero in on New Orleans; Louisiana Governor Blanco declares a state of emergency.

Aug. 29, 2005

▷ Katrina makes landfall; storm surge inundates some communities; levees fail.

Sep. 24, 2005

△ Hurricane Rita makes landfall; parts of New Orleans are flooded again.

↑ Flood waters inundating New Orleans on August 30, 2005

Feb. 28, 2006

▽ The city holds its first post-Katrina Mardi Gras.

Jan. 2007

A Dutch engineering firm commissioned to build a new flood control system.

Dec. 23, 2007

▽ St. Charles Avenue Streetcar service fully restored.

May. 6, 2006

▲ All New Orleans neighborhoods are declared officially "open for return."

Sep. 25, 2006

Mercedes-Benz Superdome reopens for the New Orleans Saints' first football game since Katrina.

EXPERIENCE

Bourbon Street buzzes with activity

UPPER FRENCH QUARTER

For many visitors, the French Quarter is synonymous with New Orleans. Founded in 1718 by Jean-Baptiste Le Moyne de Bienville, the original 20 blocks of Nouvelle-Orléans were laid out here on a grid pattern in 1721. Under Spanish rule, in the late 18th century, the district developed as a hub of trade, and the landmark Cathedral, Cabildo, and Presbytère formed the civic and religious heart of the colony.

The Louisiana Purchase of 1803 ushered in a golden age of economic and cultural growth, but following the Civil War, the quarter declined, and many wealthy merchants moved elsewhere. By the 20th century, the French Quarter's crumbling landmarks were in need of repair, but cheap rents attracted writers and artists, lending the area its alternative ambience.

The Upper French Quarter is the heart of the district. The neighborhood escaped Hurricane Katrina with little wind or flood damage, and remains an example of quintessential New Orleans architecture, with pretty Creole cottages and Spanish-style lacy galleries. Retaining its beautiful streetscapes and romantic atmosphere, the Vieux Carré (old square) is home to upscale restaurants, busy bars, and glittering antique shops, with musicians playing on every street corner.

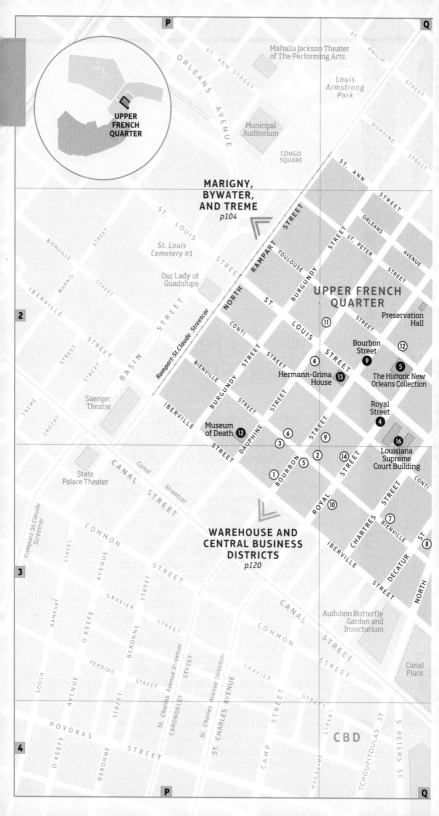

UPPER FRENCH QUARTER

Must Sees
1. St. Louis Cathedral
2. The Presbytère
3. The Cabildo
4. Royal Street
5. The Historic New Orleans Collection
6. Steamboat *Natchez*

Experience More
7. Jackson Square
8. The 1850 House
9. Bourbon Street
10. Pontalba Buildings
11. Père Antoine Alley and St. Anthony's Garden
12. Museum of Death
13. Hermann-Grima House
14. Le Petit Theatre
15. Pirate's Alley
16. Louisiana Supreme Court Building
17. New Orleans Pharmacy Museum
18. Napoleon House
19. Jean Lafitte National Historical Park Visitor Center

Eat
1. Galatoire's
2. R'Evolution
3. GW Fins
4. Bayona

Drink
5. Old Absinthe House
6. Arnaud's French 75 Bar
7. The Chart Room
8. Beachbum Berry's Latitude 29

Stay
9. Royal Sonesta New Orleans
10. Hotel Monteleone
11. Audubon Cottages
12. Maison de Ville

Shop
13. M.S. Rau Antiques
14. Keil's Antiques

0 meters 250
0 yards 250

N

ST. LOUIS CATHEDRAL

📍 Q2 🚪 Jackson Square 🚋 St. Charles Ave and Canal streetcars
🚌 5, 55, 81 🕙 10am–4:30pm daily 🌐 saintlouiscathedral.org

Dedicated to King Louis IX of France, St. Louis is the oldest continuously active Roman Catholic cathedral in the country. New Orleans' most recognizable landmark, the cathedral towers over Jackson Square, its mix of Spanish and French Neo-Gothic architecture a stately illustration of its history.

Two earlier churches once stood on this site: the first, a wooden church built in 1718, was destroyed by a hurricane in 1722; and the second, more robust construction was erected in 1727, but consumed by the great fire of 1788 that destroyed much of the French Quarter. The church was rebuilt by the Spanish from 1789, and made a cathedral in 1794. Restorations continued through the early 19th century, some to designs by renowned architect J. N. B. de Pouilly – as such, the cathedral as it stands today reveals little of its original Spanish structure. It is flanked by the most important buildings of the early colony, the Cabildo and the Presbytère, both former seats of Spanish government. The breathtaking interior is well maintained by the Archdiocese of New Orleans.

↑ The cathedral's grand interior, decorated with Baroque murals

← Elaborate stained-glass windows adorning the basilica

The carved-wood Baroque altars were constructed in Ghent, Belgium, and brought to the cathedral in pieces.

A great mural of St. Louis announcing the Seventh Crusade.

Stained-glass windows with figures of Catholic saints adorn the cathedral's interior.

The steeples, portico, and pilasters were added in 1851.

Ceiling murals by Alsatian artist Erasme Humbrecht (1872) portray biblical stories.

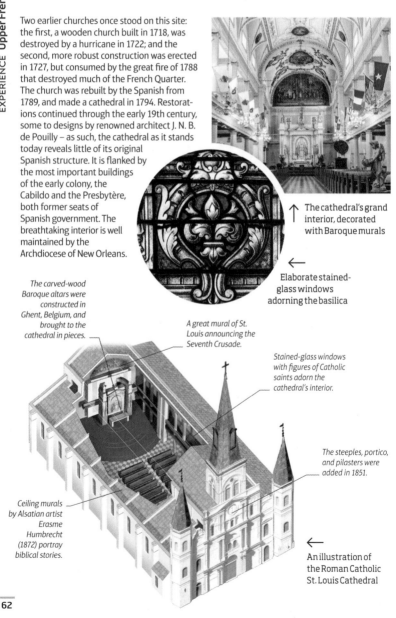

← An illustration of the Roman Catholic St. Louis Cathedral

Did You Know?

Cast in Paris, the cathedral's clock bell "Victoire" has tolled hourly since 1819.

↑ St. Louis Cathedral presiding over Jackson Square, flanked by the Presbytère and the Cabildo

❷ 🏛

THE PRESBYTÈRE

📍Q2 🏠751 Chartres street 🚋St. Charles Ave and Canal streetcars
🚌5, 55, 81 🕐10am-4:30pm Tue-Sun 🌐louisianastatemuseum.org

Set proudly alongside St. Louis Cathedral, overlooking Jackson Square, the Presbytère was constructed in 1794 as a complement to the Cabildo. A National Historic Landmark since 1970, today the site forms part of the Louisiana State Museum.

→
Seahorse costume on display in the Mardi Gras exhibit

This striking building was designed in 1791 by Gilbeto Guillemard (1747–1808), intended to serve as a rectory to the adjacent cathedral (p62). First known as the Casa Curial (Ecclesiastical House), the Presbytère was sited on the former residence or "presbytery" of Capuchin monks, from which it derives its French name. The building's construction was complicated by the sudden death of its financer Don Andres Almonaster y Rojas, in 1798. In 1805, wardens of the cathedral took control of construction, and the building was completed in 1813.

The Louisiana Supreme Court was housed here until 1853, when the church sold the building to the city. The city's civil courts occupied the Presbytère until 1910. The property was transferred to the Louisiana State Museum in 1908, and the Presbytère opened to the public in 1911.

Today, the Presbytère holds two permanent exhibits, the first focusing on hurricanes Katrina and Rita, and their impact on Louisiana. The second collection celebrates the festival of Mardi Gras, exploring its origins in 18th-century Louisiana through to the jubilant festivities enjoyed in New Orleans today.

Did You Know?

Hurricane Rita followed just four weeks after Katrina – both storms reached Category 5 at sea.

MUSEUM GUIDE

Two large permanent exhibitions are installed on the first and second floors, showing different ent sides of New Orleans' culture. On the first floor, "Living with Hurricanes: Katrina and Beyond" explores the impact of the 2005 hurricanes on the city of New Orleans, with moving eyewitness accounts, interactive displays, and movies. On the second floor is a vivid celebration of carnival – "Mardi Gras: It's Carnival Time in Louisiana" – with costumes, ball gowns, and pieces of brightly colored floats among the collections.

←

Louisiana residents sharing their experiences of Katrina and Rita

1 The imposing exterior of the Presbytère and St. Louis Cathedral, illuminated at night.

2 Cajun costumes and memorabilia are set on display in the museum's Mardi Gras collection.

3 "Living with Hurricanes" exhibits explore the levee system protecting the city.

MARDI GRAS

Each year, New Orleans' Carnival attracts over a million visitors. Since the 1700s, the period between Twelfth Night (January 6) and Ash Wednesday (the start of Lent) has been celebrated with lavish balls presented by private citizen groups known as "krewes." The first such group was the Mystic Krewe of Comus, founded in 1856 – it was soon joined by Rex (1872), and Proteus (1882). New krewes continue to emerge today, with membership open to members' relatives, or for a fee. As well as private balls, krewes put on public parades with ornate costumes and floats, which take place for 10 days before Mardi Gras.

PARADE FLOATS

Each krewe has 14 or more colorful floats, some still made of traditional papier-mâché, that are pulled through the city during the parades. Many floats are constructed at Blaine Kern's Mardi Gras World and can be seen there all year long (p149). The Presbytère (p64) presents a colorful display of Mardi Gras floats and history.

MARDI GRAS COLORS

The purple, green, and gold Carnival decorations derive from a costume worn by the king of Carnival, "Rex," during an 1872 parade. Today, these colors symbolize justice (purple), faith (green), and power (gold), and adorn throws (souvenir trinkets tossed from the floats), like doubloons, beads, and dolls. The traditional food of Carnival, king cake is decorated with Mardi Gras colors, and contains a small plastic figure of a baby, representing the baby Jesus.

↑ Rich cinnamon king cake adorned with frosting and a plastic baby Jesus

MARDI GRAS INDIANS

The Mardi Gras Indians form a secretive but significant part of the Carnival celebrations. Their parades began in the late 19th century, when members from African American communities processed through the backstreets of Mardi Gras. With their exuberantly beaded costumes, feathered headdresses, and krewes named after imaginary "tribes," these groups pay homage to the American Indians who once hid runaway slaves. Mardi Gras Indians can also be spotted parading at Jazz Fest (p172) and on St. Joseph's Day, and their traditions are explored at the Backstreet Cultural Museum in Treme (p115).

→ The Parade of Rex processing along Canal Street, and (inset) Mardi Gras Indians celebrating in beaded costumes

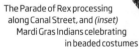

PARADE KREWES

① Krewe of Muses
Named for the ancient Greek daughters of Zeus, Muses is one of the few all-female krewes. They delight crowds by throwing lavishly decorated shoes on their route.

② Krewe of Bacchus
The Bacchus Parade on the Sunday before Mardi Gras features more than 25 floats, including some of the largest and longest, such as the heralded "Bacchagator."

③ Krewe of Zulu Parade
The Zulu Social Aid and Pleasure Club produces this festive parade, held on the morning of Mardi Gras, just before Rex. One of the most famous Krewe of Zulu carnival kings was Louis Armstrong, crowned in 1949.

④ Krewe of Rex Parade
The crown jewel of New Orleans' Mardi Gras is the Krewe of Rex Parade which first appeared in 1872. Each year Rex crowns a prominent New Orleanian the "king" of Mardi Gras.

⑤ Krewe of Armenius Gay Mardi Gras Ball
The LGBT+ community produces some of the most elaborate Mardi Gras balls: Armenius throws fabulous, uproariously funny balls.

3 🖊️ Ⓜ️

THE CABILDO

📍 Q2 🏠 701 Chartres street 🚋 St. Charles Ave and Canal streetcars
🚌 5, 55, 81 🕐 10am-4:30pm Tue-Sun 🌐 louisianastatemuseum.org

Set beside St. Louis Cathedral and the Presbytère, the Cabildo is
the third in the trio of buildings framing the north of Jackson Square.
Now a museum, this landmark houses exhibits that delve into the
colorful and turbulent history of the city.

The original Cabildo building was destroyed
by the great French Quarter fire of 1788. The
structure seen today was rebuilt and financed
by Don Andrés Almonaster y Rojas in 1794. It
served as a capitol for the legislative assembly
of the Spanish colonial government, then
as the City Hall.

Following the Louisiana Purchase of
1803 (p50), a December 20 ceremony was
held in the Cabildo to mark France's transfer
of the territory to the U.S. From 1853 to 1910,
the Cabildo housed the state Supreme Court.
Landmark court cases, such as the Plessy v.
Ferguson case of 1896 (p52) were held here
in the Sala Capitular (Meeting Room).

Today, the Cabildo forms part of the
Louisiana State Museum (LSM). Collections
include a permanent display on the Battle
of New Orleans, and rotating exhibitions that
delve into the history and culture of Louisiana.

↑ Exploring interactive exhibits
about the Battle of New Orleans

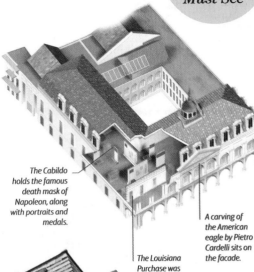

→
The Cabildo, set beside
St. Louis Cathedral
on Jackson Square

> 💬 **INSIDER TIP**
> **Friendly Crowd**
>
> Join Friends of the
> Cabildo, a volunteer-run
> group that supports the
> LSM, on their fascinat-
> ing walking tours of the
> French Quarter, held
> daily at 10:30am and
> 1:30pm *(www.friends
> ofthecabildo.org)*.

*The Cabildo
holds the famous
death mask of
Napoleon, along
with portraits and
medals.*

*A carving of
the American
eagle by Pietro
Cardelli sits on
the facade.*

*The Louisiana
Purchase was
signed in the
Sala Capitular.*

←
The impressive 18th-century
Cabildo overlooking busy
Jackson Square

TOP 4 COLLECTION PIECES

**Napoleon's
Death Mask**
This rare bronze cast of
the French Emperor's
face was made after his
death in 1821.

**The Battle of
New Orleans (1839)**
Awe-inspiring
painting of the Battle
of New Orleans by
Eugene Louis Lami
(1800–1890).

The Iberville Stone
A chunk of marble
placed by the French-
Canadian explorer,
Iberville to mark the
location of the new
French colony in
Biloxi in 1699.

**Carte de la
Louisiane (1718)**
Guillaume de L'Isle's map
was printed in two
editions; the second
locates New Orleans.

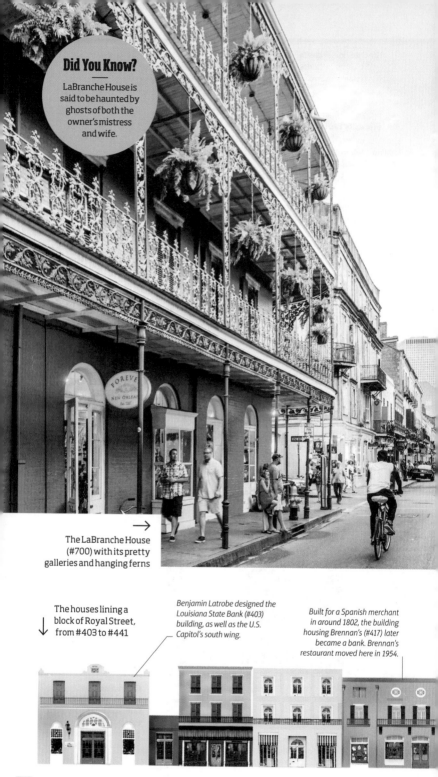

Did You Know?

LaBranche House is said to be haunted by ghosts of both the owner's mistress and wife.

→
The LaBranche House (#700) with its pretty galleries and hanging ferns

The houses lining a block of Royal Street, ↓ from #403 to #441

Benjamin Latrobe designed the Louisiana State Bank (#403) building, as well as the U.S. Capitol's south wing.

Built for a Spanish merchant in around 1802, the building housing Brennan's (#417) later became a bank. Brennan's restaurant moved here in 1954.

4

ROYAL STREET

Q2 **St. Charles Ave** **5, 55, 81, 82**

Running through the historic heart of the city, Royal Street is the pride of the French Quarter. Many of its beautiful buildings date back to the 18th century, when the thoroughfare was the city's financial center and most fashionable street. Today, this pretty parade is alive with shops, restaurants, and bars, along with galleries and museums.

Aside from the many fine antiques shops and restaurants that pepper Royal Street, many of the handsome landmarks here have been transformed into museums and galleries: at #533, the Historic New Orleans Collection occupies a complex of houses built in 1792 *(p72)* and at #541 you'll find the Galerie d'Art Français, showcasing contemporary French art. Meanwhile #700, LaBranche House, which was constructed in 1835 for sugar planter Jean Baptiste LaBranche, is among the city's most photographed buildings, known as it is for its fine oak-leaf ironwork and attractive hanging ferns.

↑ A quartet of street musicians providing open-air entertainment on Royal Street

SHOP

M. S. Rau Antiques
Established in 1912, M. S. Rau is internationally renowned for its range of antique furniture and objets d'art.

Q2
630 Royal Street
rauantiques.com

Keil's Antiques
A family-run business dating from 1899, Keil's stocks superb antique jewelry, as well as chandeliers, furniture, and mirrors.

Q3
325 Royal Street
keilsantiques.com

Moss Antiques (#411) offers a fine range of French antiques.

The cocktail was born at Antoine Peychaud's Pharmacy (#437) when pharmacist Antoine Peychaud mixed brandy with his bitters and served the potion in a coquetier (egg cup).

5 ⚡ 🅜 🖵 🛍

THE HISTORIC NEW ORLEANS COLLECTION

📍 Q2 🏠 Merieult House: 533 Royal Street; Seignouret-Brulatour Building and Tricentennial Wing: 520 Royal Street; Williams Research Center: 410 Chartres Street 🚋 St. Charles Ave 🚌 55, 81, 82 🕐 9:30am–4:30pm Tue–Sat, 10:30am–4:30pm Sun 🚫 Public hols 🖥 hnoc.org

Founded in 1966, this vast collection of photographs, prints, paintings, and artifacts is a comprehensive record of New Orleans' history and culture going back more than 300 years. The works are on display at several historic French Quarter buildings.

What began as a personal collection of materials gathered by local couple General and Mrs. L. Kemper Williams has become the pre-eminent treasury of archives on the city. The works are housed in 18th- and 19th-century premises across three campuses in the French Quarter. Merieult House features more than ten galleries of historical artifacts such as maps, paintings, and furnishings. The Williams Research Center holds the collection's archives, while the Seignouret-Brulatour Building houses a permanent gallery dedicated to the history of the French Quarter.

Did You Know?

The Historic New Orleans Collection encompasses over one million artifacts.

1 The Reading Room at the Williams Research Center is an invaluable local resource.

2 The facade of Merieult House at 533 Royal Street, which holds the Louisiana History Galleries and the Williams Gallery.

3 *Portrait of Lydia Brown* (1922-28) by Josephine Marien Crawford is displayed in the French Quarter Gallery's Art and Literature Collection.

← The sumptuous interior of the Counting House, and *(inset)* the tranquil inner courtyard, Royal Street's Merieult House Campus

TOUR THE COLLECTIONS

Four guided tours of the collections are available. The first, the Architecture and Courtyard Tour, highlights the various styles on display around the Royal Street campus. The Williams Residence Tour explores the collectors' late 19th-century Italianate townhouse. The third tour is of the Exhibition Center at 520 Royal Street, where visitors learn about the architecture and history of the buildings housing the permanent galleries and temporary exhibits. Each December, the Collection lavishly decorates the Williams residence in mid-20th-century style, and gives its special "Holiday Home" tour.

STEAMBOAT NATCHEZ

R3 **Woldenberg Riverfront Park wharf** **45, 87** **Harbor jazz cruises 11:30am and 2:30pm daily, dinner jazz cruise 7pm daily** **steamboatnatchez.com**

For a reminder of the old days of river travel, take a two-hour trip on the Steamboat *Natchez* – pride of the riverfront in downtown New Orleans – and cruise along the Mississippi in style with a swinging soundtrack of jazz.

Ninth of its name, this incarnation of the *Natchez* has been sailing since 1975, but her original steam engines and steering system were built in 1925. In the 19th century, steamboats traveled the length of the Mississippi, taking between three and five days to get from Louisville, Kentucky, to New Orleans. The boatmen were notorious brawlers who went looking for women and liquor at the end of a trip and established New Orleans' reputation as the "City of Sin." In their heyday, from 1830 to 1860, some 30 steamboats lined up at the levee. The steamboat era ended by the close of the 19th century with the development of railroads and highways. Today, the *Natchez* can be seen gliding along the river on daily two-hour jazz-cruises, and every so often, competing in a paddle steamer race.

> **GREAT VIEW**
> **Steam Player**
>
> Breathtaking skyline views are possible a few minutes into the river tour on this steamboat. Head to the Hurricane Deck after setting off and you should be able to spy most of New Orleans' downtown.

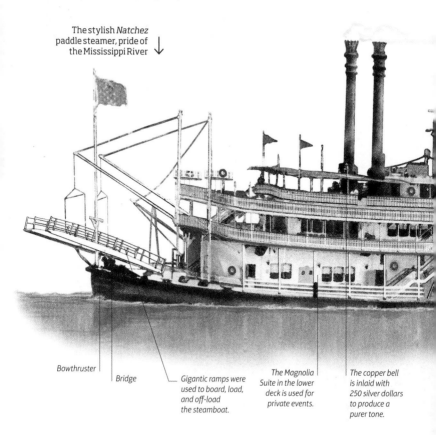

The stylish *Natchez* paddle steamer, pride of the Mississippi River ↓

Bowthruster

Bridge

Gigantic ramps were used to board, load, and off-load the steamboat.

The Magnolia Suite in the lower deck is used for private events.

The copper bell is inlaid with 250 silver dollars to produce a purer tone.

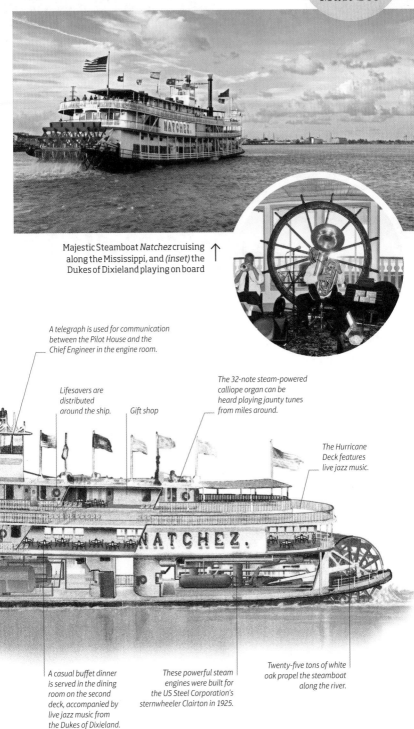

Majestic Steamboat *Natchez* cruising along the Mississippi, and *(inset)* the Dukes of Dixieland playing on board ↑

A telegraph is used for communication between the Pilot House and the Chief Engineer in the engine room.

Lifesavers are distributed around the ship.

Gift shop

The 32-note steam-powered calliope organ can be heard playing jaunty tunes from miles around.

The Hurricane Deck features live jazz music.

A casual buffet dinner is served in the dining room on the second deck, accompanied by live jazz music from the Dukes of Dixieland.

These powerful steam engines were built for the US Steel Corporation's sternwheeler Clairton in 1925.

Twenty-five tons of white oak propel the steamboat along the river.

EXPERIENCE MORE

7

Jackson Square

Q2 **Riverfront** **5, 55**

Today, an attractive and lively meeting place, this square was named the Place d'Armes in the early French colony, when it was little more than a muddy field. Here, the troops were drilled, criminals were placed in the stocks, and executions were carried out. In 1850, it was renamed for the hero of the Battle of New Orleans (p50), after the Baroness Pontalba laid out the gardens and pathways of the square in a radial pattern, with walkways stemming out from the center. Under her auspices, the Pelanne brothers designed the handsome wrought-iron fence that encloses the square. At the center stands a statue of General Andrew Jackson astride a rearing horse. The inscription "The Union must and shall be preserved" on the plinth was added by General Benjamin "Beast" Butler, when he occupied the city during the American Civil War (p52). Today, there are plenty of

benches where visitors can sit and enjoy the charm of the historical houses that surround the square. Outside the park, artists rent space and hang their works on the enclosing fence, and on the flagstones around the square, tarot card readers, jazz players, and clowns entertain visitors throughout the week.

8

The 1850 House

R2 **523 St. Ann St**
524-9118 **5, 55**
10am-4:30pm Tue-Sun
Public hols

Situated in the residence above the Lower Pontalba Building, the 1850 House is the Louisiana State Museum's faithful recreation of a mid-nineteenth-century antebellum apartment. Accessed by a dramatic circular staircase, the bedrooms contain all the innovations of their day, including walk-in closets and private bathrooms. Also displayed are decorative arts and everyday artifacts of the period.

TOP 3 FRENCH QUARTER HISTORICAL FIGURES

Jean-Baptiste le Moyne de Bienville (1680-1767)
French-Canadian founder of "La Nouvelle Orleans" (1718) who oversaw the French Quarter's design.

Micaela Almonester, Baroness de Pontalba (1795-1874)
Creole aristocrat, entrepreneur, and property developer whose name graces the Pontalba Buildings.

Andrew Jackson (1767-1845)
Divisive seventh U.S. president and figurehead of the South who, as a general during the American Revolutionary War, defeated the British in the Battle of New Orleans in 1815.

←
Artists displaying colorful works in busy Jackson Square

9
Bourbon Street

🚩 Q2 🚋 Canal 🚌 100, 114

Its reputation as a party hub aside, this legendary street's name has nothing to do with the whiskey, despite the string of bars lining the thoroughfare; rather, it refers to the French royal family of Bourbon. While its infamy is not entirely unearned (during Mardi Gras, the lacy balconies above the sidewalks sag from the weight of drunken revelers), Bourbon Street is great for dining, architecture, and music. At No. 733, the intimate **Fritzel's Jazz Club** has attracted the best musicians since 1969, and just a few minutes walk away, **Preservation Hall** has helped preserve New Orleans jazz since its inception in 1961, still hosting top-quality jazz night after night.

Fritzel's Jazz Club

🚩 Q2 🏠 733 Bourbon St
📞 504-586-4800

Preservation Hall

♿ 🚩 Q2 🏠 726 St. Peters St 🌐 preservationhall.com

10 💻 🛍️
Pontalba Buildings

🚩 Q2 🏠 St. Peter & St. Ann Sts 🚋 Riverfront 🚌 5, 55

In 1848, Baroness Pontalba (Micaela Almonester) supervised the building of these block-long apartments flanking the uptown and downtown sides of Jackson Square. They were built at a cost of just over $300,000, and at the time considered the best and largest apartments of their kind.

At the age of 15, Micaela had married the foppish aristocrat Celestin Pontalba, a distant cousin, and moved to Paris. There, her father-in-law tried to force her to sign over her entire estate. When she refused, he attempted to kill her, but only succeeded in shooting off two of her fingers.

She courageously separated from her husband in 1848 and returned to New Orleans. The baroness, like her father, the philanthropist Don Andrés Almonester y Rojas, was a developer. With plans brought back from Paris, she proceeded to build apartments like the ones she had seen in Paris. The design of the initials A and P (for Almonester and Pontalba) in the cast-iron railings of the buildings' galleries is attributed to one of the baroness's sons, an artist.

EAT

Galatoire's
This century-old institution serves up French Creole classics in its elegant dining room. Friday lunchtimes are one of the city's most decadent traditions, and dressing up is essential.

🚩 P3 🏠 209 Bourbon St
🌐 galatoires.com

$$$

R'Evolution
Elegant, mural-clad dining room in the Royal Sonesta Hotel. Expect whimsical, innovative takes on Southern cuisine, including gumbo and beignets.

🚩 P2 🏠 777 Bienville St
🌐 revolutionnola.com

$$$

GW Fins
The menu changes almost daily at this classy seafood spot, giving fish a truly original head-to-tail treatment.

🚩 P2 🏠 808 Bienville St
🌐 gwfins.com

$$$

Bayona
Charming, cosy Creole cottage setting with a romantic ambience. The menu spans the globe, from American classics to Asian and European.

🚩 P2 🏠 430 Dauphine St
🌐 bayona.com

$$$

←
The Parisian-style Pontalba apartment buildings overlooking Jackson Square

STAY

Royal Sonesta
An oasis of Art Deco décor and contemporary art amid the Bourbon Street clamour. Visit its destination restaurant (R'Evolution), 19th-century carriage house bar, and atmospheric jazz venue.

 Q2 🏠300 Bourbon St
🌐sonesta.com

$$⑤

Hotel Monteleone
An independent, fifth-generation run hotel dating back to the 19th century. It is famed for its traditional style, literary associations (Faulkner and Capote drank here), and rotating Carousel bar.

Q3 🏠215 Royal St
🌐hotelmonteleone.com

$$⑤

Audubon Cottages
With its private gardens and butler service, Audubon is one of the most discreet and luxurious properties in the city, once favored by Elizabeth Taylor.

Q2 🏠509 Dauphine St
🌐auduboncottages.com

$$$

Maison de Ville
A boutique property, recently revamped to recapture the romance of its glory days in the 1960s. The rooms are replete with antiques and the tranquil courtyard is a delight.

 Q2 🏠727 Toulouse St
🌐maisondeville.com

$$$

↑ The tranquil St. Anthony's Garden, set out beneath St. Louis Cathedral

⑪ Père Antoine Alley and St. Anthony's Garden

Q2 🚊Riverfront 🚌5, 55

This alley is named for one of the city's most beloved clergymen, Father Antonio de Sedella (Père Antoine), who served as pastor of St. Louis Cathedral for 40 years. He was admired for his compassionate ministry to the poor, whom he assiduously fed and clothed.

The fenced garden, once a dueling ground, features a great sculpture of the Sacred Heart. In the early morning and evening, the scent of sweet olives lingers in the air.

⑫ Museum of Death

P2 🏠227 Dauphine St
🚌5 🕙10am-7pm daily
🌐museumofdeath.net/nola

This museum is not for the fainthearted or for families with young children. For those with a strong stomach and an interest in the many aspects of mortality, it offers a macabre collection, including skulls and coffins, apparatus used by morticians, crime and morgue scenes, and even artworks and letters from infamous serial killers. A real

shrunken head, graphic car accident photographs, and newspaper front pages recording momentous and tragic moments in American and world history also feature in the fascinating collection. There's a stunning array of taxidermy, as well as a skeleton of an alligator chewing on a human leg bone.

The museum's exhibits are constantly evolving and its owners are always looking out for new and interesting local artifacts and stories. New Orleans is a city with a special relationship to death, and while this museum isn't for everyone, its presence here is appropriate.

---

⑬   Hermann-Grima House

Q2 🏠820 St. Louis St 🚌5
🕙10am-4pm daily; tours 10am-3pm Thu-Tue
🚫Public hols 🌐hgghh.org

This gabled brick house stands out because it is one of the few examples of American Federal-style architecture in the French Quarter. William Brand built it in 1831 for Samuel Hermann, a German-Jewish merchant. He lost his fortune in 1837 and had to sell the house to Judge Felix Grima. The house features a central doorway with a fanlight and marble

THE HISTORY OF THE FRENCH QUARTER

This historic district was founded in 1718 by Montrealer naval officer Jean Baptiste Bienville. In 1762 Louis XV of France gave the quarter to Charles III of Spain, and the district developed as a hub of trade under Spanish rule. Under the Louisiana Purchase of 1803 it was transferred to the United States. The Civil War hailed the end of New Orlean's golden era and the decline of the French Quarter. By the 20th century, the district's crumbling historic buildings were in need of repair, and in 1936 the Vieux Carré Commission was created to restore their former glory.

steps. Inside, the floors and doors are made of cypress, and the rooms feature elegant marble fireplaces. The three-story service quarters, located in a separate building off the parterre behind the house, feature former slave quarters and a kitchen containing a rare four-burner wood-fired stove with a beehive oven.

14

Le Petit Theatre

📍 Q2 🏠 616 St. Peter St
🚌 5, 55 🕐 Noon-5pm
Mon-Fri & show days)
🌐 lepetittheatre.com

This tiny theater was the brainchild of the Drawing Room Players, a group of actors who came together in 1916 under the management of Mrs. Oscar Nixon. Their first theater was located in the Lower Pontalba Building, but the current site was bought in 1922 and was used for the first American productions of Eugene O'Neill's *Beyond the Horizon* and Oscar Wilde's *Lady Windermere's Fan*. A beguiling courtyard with a fountain sits in the center of the building. Legend has it that the fountain is haunted by the spirit of a jilted bride.

In 2011, part of the building was converted into an eatery. Tableau is part of the famous Dickie Brennan & Co. group of restaurants, and guests can choose between dining in the courtyard or on the balcony overlooking Jackson Square.

The theater hosts a season of performances from September to June, and acts as a headquarters during the Tennessee Williams New Orleans Literary Festival and Writers' Conference in March.

15

Pirate's Alley

📍 Q2 🚌 5, 55

Although there is no concrete evidence, the most popular theory is that this narrow cobbled row, extending alongside St Louis Cathedral, was once the favorite haunt of the infamous pirate brothers Jean and Pierre Lafitte.

Today, the alley attracts visitors with its bohemian atmosphere and open-air cafés and shops. At 624 is Faulkner House Books, in the building where William Faulkner wrote his first novel, *Soldier's Pay*, in 1925. Today, the store's shelves are lined with Faulkner first editions as well as works by other major Southern authors. Next door is Pirate's Alley Café, which stands on the site of a former Spanish colonial prison, built in 1769.

↑ Faulkner House Books at 624 Pirate Alley, once the residence of William Faulkner

Did You Know?

Many of Louisiana's current state laws are descended from the civil code first devised by Napoleon.

16

Louisiana Supreme Court Building

Q2 **400 Royal St** **Riverfront** **5** **9am–5pm Mon–Fri** **Public hols** **lasc.org**

When this massive granite and marble structure was built in 1908–10, the French Quarter was on the downslide. Erecting this splendid Beaux Arts court building was an early exercise in urban renewal. Despite a few protests, an entire block of historic 18th- and early 19th-century buildings was razed to make way for it. The Louisiana Supreme Court occupied it from 1910 to 1958. Thereafter, it began to decline and massive trees were planted on site to conceal the building's exterior. It was then home to a string of state agencies, none of which kept up the maintenance on this architecturally intricate structure. In the 1990s, the state finally launched a renovation program, and since 2004, the building has once again served as the home of the Louisiana Supreme Court, the Louisiana Law Library, and other state legal offices. A small museum on the first floor includes exhibits on the development of Louisiana law.

Browsing the ↑ collections of the Pharmacy Museum, and *(inset)* the museum's historic storefront

17

New Orleans Pharmacy Museum

Q2 **514 Chartres St** **5, 55, 81** **10am–4pm Tue–Sat** **Public hols** **pharmacymuseum.org**

This museum is located on the site of the first licensed pharmacy in the United States, operated by Louis Joseph Dufilho from 1823 to 1855. The original display cases and mahogany cabinets contain some gruesome-looking early surgical tools – saws, knives, and bloodletting instruments – as well as herbal remedies, many of which were forerunners of today's drugs. These include a bottle of salicin, an early form of aspirin produced by Bayer & Co. from black willow bark. The Pharmacy Museum also features a splendid 1855 marble soda fountain at which appealing sodas were first concocted to

↑ The imposing facade of the Louisiana Supreme Court Building,

and for a warm version of the muffuletta, a traditional New Orleans deli sandwich (p26). It occupies two buildings, one of which is a two-story structure, built in 1798, facing St. Louis Street; the second, built in 1814, is a three-story building with a mezzanine. Together, they were the home of Mayor Nicholas Girod, who planned to free Napoleon from imprisonment on St. Helena Island. With the help of Dominique You and a pirate band, Girod intended to bring him to this refuge, but Napoleon died before the mission could be undertaken. Today, the walls of the house are adorned with all kinds of Napoleonic decor and memorabilia. Both buildings are attributed to leading New Orleans architect and artist Jean-Hyacinthe Laclotte, and the balcony railings were crafted by prolific blacksmith William Malus. The cupola on the roof is a New Orleans landmark.

Jean Laﬁtte National Historical Park Visitor Center

📍 Q3 🏠 419 Decatur St 🚌 5, 55, 81 🕙 9am–4:30pm Tue-Sat 🚫 Dec 25, Mardi Gras 🌐 nps.gov/jela

The Jean Laﬁtte National Historical Park comprises a network of six historically and culturally significant Louisiana sites, including three in Cajun Country (p194) and the Chalmette Battlefield (p127). This visitor center has some rather excellent displays on the geography, history, and culture of the Mississippi River Delta region, including dioramas and interactive exhibits. It also offers slide shows and ranger-led walking tours of the French Quarter at 9:30 every morning.

help the medicine go down. The second floor features a 19th-century sick room, a fine collection of eye glasses, homeopathic remedies, and an impressive collection of 19th-century dental instruments. The walled courtyard garden is filled with medicinal herbs.

Napoleon House

📍 Q2 🏠 500 Chartres St 🚌 5, 55, 81 🕙 11am-10pm Sun-Thu, 11am-11pm Fri & Sat 🌐 napoleonhouse.com

One of the city's most atmospheric bars, Napoleon House is famous for its Pimm's Cup

DRINK

Old Absinthe House

This bar dates back to 1807, when pirates and ne'er-do-wells drank within its storied walls. Today it's a lively Bourbon Street spot, and one of the few places in the city with a full absinthe service.

📍 P3 🏠 240 Bourbon St 📞 523-3181

Arnaud's French 75 Bar

This bijoux annex to Arnaud's Restaurant oozes old-world charm, and serves up mouth-watering versions of the eponymous French 75 cocktail, a refreshing champagne and gin mix.

📍 P2 🏠 240 Bourbon St 🌐 arnauds restaurant.com

The Chart Room

A true French Quarter dive bar, open 24 hours and specializing in cheap drinks and loud music, and giving visitors a good story to take home.

📍 Q3 🏠 300 Chartres St 📞 522-1708

Beachbum Berry's Latitude 29

Jeff "Beachbum" Berry is among the world's foremost mixologists and a figurehead of the recent tiki cocktail bar revival. Come here for phenomenal fruity, boozy concoctions in striking glassware.

📍 Q3 🏠 321 N Peters St 🌐 latitude29nola.com

A SHORT WALK
JACKSON SQUARE

Distance 0.5 miles (0.8 km) **Time** 10 minutes
Nearest Streetcar Riverfront

In the historic heart of the French Quarter, Jackson Square is surrounded by a striking and harmonious collection of buildings. This block initially served as a military parade ground, or *place d'armes*, where troops were trained and drilled, executions carried out, and public meetings held. The Cathedral, Cabildo, and Presbytère face the square. The plaza was redesigned in 1848, when Baroness Pontalba built the two elegant apartment buildings on the upriver and downriver sides of the square.

Today, the square makes a pleasant place to wander, amid performing musicians, hotdog stands, and the stalls of local artists displaying their works.

Tennesee Williams wrote A Streetcar Named Desire in an apartment at **632 St. Peter Street**.

Le Petit Theatre du Vieux Carré, *established in 1916, moved to its current location in 1919 (p79). The building is a replica of the original.*

The Omni Royal Orleans Hotel *is constructed on the site of the 1836 St. Louis Hotel.*

START

The French Quarter's beloved **Napoleon House** *bar is devoted to the emperor's memory, with portraits and other memorabilia adorning the walls.*

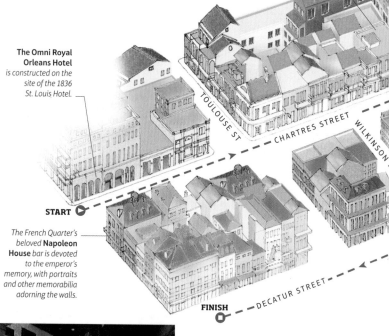

TOULOUSE ST

CHARTRES STREET

WILKINSON S

DECATUR STREET

FINISH

0 meters   50   N
0 yards   50

← Napoleon House, filled with memorabilia relating to the French emperor

Locator Map
Fore more detail see p60

← A Lucky Dogs hot dog stand sitting outside the Cabildo and St. Louis Cathedral

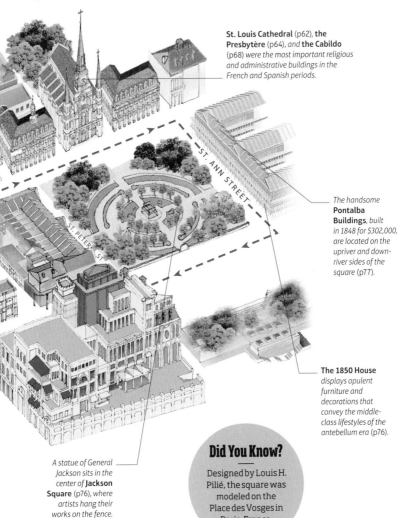

St. Louis Cathedral (p62), **the Presbytère** (p64), *and* **the Cabildo** (p68) *were the most important religious and administrative buildings in the French and Spanish periods.*

The handsome **Pontalba Buildings**, *built in 1848 for $302,000, are located on the upriver and down-river sides of the square (p77).*

The 1850 House *displays opulent furniture and decorations that convey the middle-class lifestyles of the antebellum era (p76).*

A statue of General Jackson sits in the center of **Jackson Square** *(p76), where artists hang their works on the fence.*

Did You Know?

Designed by Louis H. Pilié, the square was modeled on the Place des Vosges in Paris, France.

A LONG WALK
AROUND THE MISSISSIPPI RIVERFRONT

Distance 1 mile (1.6 km) **Time** 25 minutes (plus the 10-minute ferry ride) **Nearest Streetcar** Riverfront

New Orleans owes its very existence to the Mississippi River, one of the world's great waterways and an iconic feature on the cultural, historic, and economic landscape of America. This walk provides superb vistas from both sides of the river, explores a portion of the levee system, and, thanks to a ride on the Algiers Ferry, gives you a chance to experience its swirling waters up close. The ferry ride is brief, but offers excellent views of the New Orleans skyline and various craft that ply the river.

Begin at **Washington Artillery Park** *(p99), a raised platform with excellent views of Jackson Square (p76) and the river.*

Descend the stairs on the river side of the platform to reach the **Moon Walk** *(p99), a paved walkway named for former New Orleans mayor Maurice "Moon" Landrieu.*

JACKSON SQUARE
START

Moonwalk Riverfront Park

Pass the berth for the **Steamboat Natchez** *(p74), a paddle wheeler that offers river trips, and listen out for the music from its steam calliope organ.*

Steamboat Natchez

Woldenberg Riverfront Park

Meander through sculpture-studded **Woldenberg Riverfront Park** *(p128), where green open spaces are popular with picnickers and joggers.*

Canal Place

The area around the **Audubon Aquarium of the Americas** *(p124) is filled with marine sculptures, shaded park benches, and vendors serving refreshments.*

Audubon Aquarium of the Americas

Harrah's Casino

World Trade Center

SPANISH PLAZA

DECATUR

N PETERS ST

NORTH PETERS STREET

N FRONT ST

IBERVILLE ST

CANAL STREET

SOUTH PETERS ST

Mississippi

Did You Know?

The Spanish Plaza was gifted to New Orleans by Spain in a gesture of friendship.

If the ferry is not in dock at the terminal, take some time to explore the adjacent **Spanish Plaza** *(p129) with its fountain ringed by tile mosaics.*

The Canal-Algiers ferry departs **Canal Street Ferry Terminal** *every 30 minutes at quarter to and a quarter past the hour (p128), transporting visitors across the river to Algiers Point (p207).*

| 0 meters | 300 |
| 0 yards | 300 |

N ↑

Locator Map
For more detail see p60 and p122

← Crossing the Mississippi on the 10-minute ferry trip from Canal Street to Algiers

The ferry docks in **Old Algiers Point**, *a village established in 1719 (p128). Turn left and follow the trail of crushed shells that top the grassy levee.*

The **Algiers Courthouse** *is a grand Romanesque Revival structure built in 1896 after a devastating fire wiped out much of the neighborhood.*

Descend the set of colorfully painted concrete steps down to **Patterson Road** *and then on to Olivier Street and Pelican Avenue, each lined with colorful Creole townhouses and shotgun-style houses.*

At the end of Pelican, turn right at **Bouny Street** *and continue up to the ferry terminal for the return trip.*

PATTERSON RD

VERRETT STREET
VALLETTE STREET
BELLEVILLE STREET
OLIVIER STREET
STREET
STREET
LAVERGNE ST
MORGAN STREET

ALGIERS

Algiers Courthouse

PELICAN AVENUE
BERMUDA STREET

Dry Dock Café and Bar

FINISH

BOUNY ST
ALIX STREET
SEGUIN ST
POWDER STREET
ELIZA

The **Dry Dock Café and Bar** *opposite the ferry terminal offers gumbo, po'boys, and a friendly atmosphere.*

→ Distinctive colorfully painted shotgun houses in Algiers

LOWER FRENCH QUARTER

Featuring handsome Creole-style houses and ornate ironwork galleries, this is the more residential part of the French Quarter. It extends from beyond St. Ann Street to Esplanade Avenue, which, in the 19th century, housed the aristocratic French Creole community. This area is home to some of the city's oldest buildings, such as the Old Ursuline Convent, dating from 1752, the only remaining French Colonial structure in New Orleans.

To the south of this quarter, the area that surrounds the French Market has long been a place for meeting and mixing; in the city's early days, it was an American Indian trading post on the banks of the Mississippi. Under French then Spanish colonial rule, the area flourished. Imported goods flowed in from overseas, and African, German, Italian, and Irish traders set up market stalls to sell their wares. In the 19th century, nearby Gallatin Street (now French Market Place) became the quarter's most notorious thoroughfare, its dimly lit brothels and disreputable saloons tempting visiting sailors.

The French Market still throngs with activity, but today makes a pleasant spot to browse for local souvenirs, fresh produce, and sizzling street food. There are plenty of bars here too, including Lafitte's Blacksmith Shop, the city's oldest. The surrounding residential streets, lined with historic houses, afford calm respite from the crowds.

LOWER FRENCH QUARTER

Must Sees
1 French Market

Experience More
2 Old Ursuline Convent
3 New Orleans Jazz National Historical Park
4 New Orleans Jazz Museum
5 Beauregard-Keyes House
6 Soniat House
7 Gallier House
8 Latrobe House
9 Lalaurie House
10 Café du Monde
11 Gauche Villa
12 Central Grocery
13 Esplanade Avenue
14 Lafitte's Blacksmith Shop
15 Cornstalk Fence
16 Madame John's Legacy
17 Washington Artillery Park and Moon Walk

Eat
① Mister Gregory's
② Verti Marte
③ Coop's Place

Drink
④ Bar Tonique
⑤ Cane and Table
⑥ Molly's at the Market
⑦ Meauxbar

Stay
⑧ Lamothe House
⑨ Inn on the Ursulines
⑩ Lafitte Guest House

Shop
⑪ Fifi Mahoney's

TREME

ESPLANADE AVENUE

Backstreet Cultural Museum

Mahalia Jackson Theater of The Performing Arts

Louis Armstrong Park

Municipal Auditorium

CONGO SQUARE

Rampart-St Claude Streetcar

UPPER FRENCH QUARTER
p58

Historic New Orleans Collection

Hermann-Grima House

Louisiana Supreme Court Building

State Palace Theater

CANAL STREET

Canal Streetcar

UPPER FRENCH QUARTER

Jean Lafitte National Historical Park Visitor Center

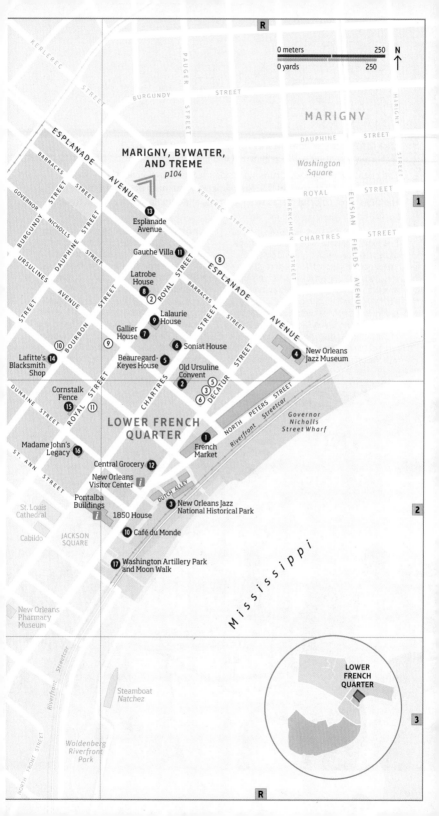

MARIGNY, BYWATER, AND TREME
p104

13 Esplanade Avenue

11 Gauche Villa

2 Latrobe House
8

9 Lalaurie House

7 Gallier House
9

6 Soniat House

5 Beauregard-Keyes House

10 Bourbon
14 Lafitte's Blacksmith Shop

2 Old Ursuline Convent

4 New Orleans Jazz Museum

15 Cornstalk Fence

11

5 Decatur
3
6

LOWER FRENCH QUARTER

16 Madame John's Legacy

12 Central Grocery

New Orleans Visitor Center

1 French Market

3 New Orleans Jazz National Historical Park

Pontalba Buildings

1850 House

10 Café du Monde

17 Washington Artillery Park and Moon Walk

St. Louis Cathedral

Cabildo

JACKSON SQUARE

New Orleans Pharmacy Museum

Mississippi

Steamboat *Natchez*

Waldenberg Riverfront Park

LOWER FRENCH QUARTER

MARIGNY

Washington Square

Governor Nicholls Street Wharf

0 meters 250
0 yards 250
N

❶ 🛠 🍴 ☕ 🖥 🛍

THE FRENCH MARKET

📍 R2 🚇 N Peters Street to Barracks Street 🚊 Riverfront Stops 1, 2, 3
🚌 55 🕐 9am–6pm daily 🌐 frenchmarket.org

The historic French Market runs alongside the Mississippi River, set between Jackson Square and the Old U.S. Mint. A people-watcher's paradise, it's one of the city's most colorful places to shop, stroll, and sample delicious local treats.

More than 200 years ago, American Indians first came to this riverside location to trade baskets, beads, and *filé* (ground sassafras leaves used in gumbo). As the port grew in the 1800s, the market flourished, with African American women selling coffee and *calas* (hot rice cakes), German farmers offering their produce, and Italian butchers selling meat. At the far end, the flea market stands on the site of the notorious neighborhood once called the "port of the missing men," because many men who visited the local bars and brothels were killed and disappeared. The present French Market buildings date from the 1930s and officially cover the six blocks of shops and cafés between St. Ann and Barracks streets. Inside the market is Dutch Alley, a triangular plaza with a performance tent, an artists' co-op, and the New Orleans Jazz National Historical Park (*p92*). At the open-air Farmers' Market, which begins at Ursulines Street, you can shop for Cajun spices and pralines, buy local artworks, or choose from a variety of mouthwatering snacks at the food stands.

1791
Founded in this year, the French Market is the oldest market in the United States.

1 Established in 1862, Café Du Monde is located on the south side of the market and is open 24 hours a day.

2 A garden shop in the French Market selling fresh, locally grown produce.

3 A distinctive yellow archway marks the entrance to the market, which also hosts farmers' and artisan markets on Wednesdays and Saturdays.

↑ The vibrant French Market, a great place to pick up handmade souvenirs

CREOLE TOMATO FESTIVAL

On the second weekend in June, the French Market celebrates the arrival of a local favorite: the Creole tomato. Grown in the rich alluvial soil of the river parishes, these fat, sweet fruits are the star of special dishes from crêpes to crawfish pies. This quirky festival features tomato-eating contests, a Bloody Mary Market, cooking demonstrations, live music, and more.

EXPERIENCE MORE

2

Old Ursuline Convent

📍R2 🏠1100 Chartres St
📞529-3040 🚉Riverfront
🚌55 🕐10am-4pm Mon-Fri

Dating from 1752, this convent is the oldest building in the Mississippi Valley. In the 1820s, it became the first official residence for the bishops and archbishops of New Orleans, and the home of the archdiocesan archives.

Inside the current chapel, consecrated in 1845, visitors can admire the splendid pine and cypress ceiling, Bavarian stained-glass windows, and a window depicting the Battle of New Orleans *(p50)*. A formal French garden containing a handsome iron gazebo lies in front of the building.

Neighbouring the convent, is St. Mary's Catholic Church, dating back to 1845, which has beautifully preserved statues and stained-glass windows, plus a functional Pilcher organ built in 1890.

3

New Orleans Jazz National Historical Park

📍R2 🏠916 N Peters St
🚉Riverfront 🚌5, 82
🕐10am-4:30pm Tue-Thu, 10am-4pm Fri & Sat
🌐nps.gov/jazz

The National Park Service offers seminars, films, and jazz concerts at this small visitors' center, created in 1994 to commemorate the musical legacy of New Orleans. Ranger-led walking tours of the French Quarter depart from here.

4

New Orleans Jazz Museum

📍R1 🏠400 Esplanade Ave
🚉Riverfront 🕐10am-4:30pm Tue-Sun 🌐nola jazzmuseum.org

Housed in the Old US Mint (part of the Louisiana State Museum portfolio) the

---

URSULINE NUNS

Sent by King Louis XV to set up a base to care for the poor and sick, as well as to provide education for young girls, the first Ursuline nuns journeyed to New Orleans from Rouen, France, arriving in 1727. Fourteen nuns made the arduous seven-month voyage across the Atlantic and up the Mississippi, and despite the challenging conditions on arrival, they established a school and set up a hospital, treating the slave population and wounded soldiers.

The entrance to the Old Ursuline Convent, and *(inset)* inside the convent's chapel

New Orleans Jazz Museum's comprehensive collections include rare and significant recordings, tapes, and pressings, including a 1917 disc of the first jazz recording. The instruments belonging to famous musicians, including a cornet owned by legendary Louis Armstrong, are also on display, along with photographs, paintings and prints showing the early days of jazz.

There is a live performance venue on site, where concerts, lectures, and theatrical performances are held.

Beauregard-Keyes House

📍R1 🏠1113 Chartres St
🚋Riverfront 🚌5, 55 🕐By tour only: 10am–3pm Mon-Sat hourly 🌐bkhouse.org

Twin staircases lead up to this Federal-style townhouse,

→

Central courtyard and fountain of the historic Beauregard-Keyes House

designed by architect François Correjolles in 1826. It is associated with several famous New Orleans residents, including master chess player Paul Morphy, who was born here in 1837, when it belonged to his grandfather, Joseph Le Carpentier. The house derives its name in part from Civil War confederate General P. G. T. Beauregard, who lived here briefly in 1866–7.

Frances Parkinson Keyes wrote many of her 51 novels here, and restored the property to its Victorian style. Today, many of the novelist's personal possessions are on display, along with those of the Beauregard family. The rooms are arranged around a courtyard, which contains a fountain that Keyes brought from Vermont, her home state.

EAT

Mister Gregory's

A modest café that bakes tempting pastries served along with French classics such as croque monsieur. There is also a fantastic shrimp boil here at weekends.

📍Q1 🏠806 Rampart St
🌐mistergregorys.com

$(\$)(\$)

Verti Marte

A French Quarter institution, this deli at the back of a convenience store is as casual as it gets, but the tasty po'boy sandwiches are allegedly a favorite of Brad Pitt.

📍R1 🏠1201 Royal St
📞525-4767

$(\$)(\$)

Coop's Place

The dining room may be no-frills, but the food is some of the best homestyle Cajun and Creole fare you'll taste, especially the signature jambalaya.

📍R2 🏠1109 Decatur St
🌐coopsplace.net

$(\$)(\$)

DRINK

Bar Tonique

Half craft cocktail joint, half casual neighborhood tavern, this is a perfect spot to relax after a long walk around the Vieux Carré. Sip a Dark and Stormy or an Old Fashioned in unpretentious surrounds.

📍Q1 🏠820 Rampart St
🌐bartonique.com

Cane and Table

Drinks are billed as "proto-tiki" – expect tasty precursors to daiquiris and the exotic cocktails you know and love. A Cuban ambiance permeates the menu.

📍R1 🏠1113 Decatur St
🌐caneandtable
snola.com

Molly's at the Market

Open 24 hours a day, this lively Irish bar is always buzzing. Mix with locals and curious tourists as the genial bartenders pull pints of Guinness and concoct their famous frozen Irish coffees.

📍R2 🏠1107 Decatur St
🌐mollysatthe
market.net

Meauxbar

A much-welcomed addition to the French Quarter, this bijoux bistro has modern twists on classic cocktails and an impressive small-production wine list alongside traditional fare like steak tartare.

📍Q1 🏠942 Rampart St
🌐meauxbar.com

↑ Sunlight streaming into the exquisitely furnished interior of Soniat House

⑥
Soniat House

📍R1 🏠1133 Chartres St
🚇Riverfront 🚌5, 55
🌐soniathouse.com

This historic residence was built in 1829 as a townhouse for wealthy sugar planter Joseph Soniat Dufossat and his family. Joseph was the second son of Chevalier Guy Saunhac du Fossat, who had been sent to Louisiana by Louis XV of France in 1751 to work as a military engineer.

The house combines classic Creole style – the flagstone carriageway, a courtyard, an external spiral staircase, and lacy iron galleries – with Greek Revival detail in the mantels and moldings. In the 1940s, the Nathaniel Felton family restored it completely. Today, it is a small hotel, exquisitely furnished with authentic antiques and decoration.

---

⑦
Gallier Historic House

📍R1 🏠1132 Royal St
🚌5, 55, 81 🕐10am–4pm
Thu–Tue 🚫Some public
hols 🌐hgghh.org

In 1857, James Gallier, Jr. designed this attractive residence, combining elements of Creole architecture, such as the carriageway and gallery

configurations, and American styles such as the internal halls (p101). The interior incorporated many innovations, including a hot-water and ventilation system. The kitchen was also placed inside, thanks to advances in cooking technology. Designer James Gallier, Jr. was the son of the city's renowned architect James Gallier, Sr., who designed the portico of the Louisiana State Bank building (p70), and Gallier Hall (p132).

Today, the house is part of the Hermann-Grima + Gallier Historic Houses Museum (p78). Among the rooms to visit here

→

The graceful exterior of Lalaurie House, belying its grim history

is the "sick room," a sparsely furnished room for the unwell. Many households had such a room, which was not surprising in a city that had 23 yellow fever epidemics between 1718 and 1860.

Latrobe House

R1 **721 Governor Nicholls St** **5, 55** **To the public**

When Benjamin Henry Latrobe designed this building in 1814, with its sturdy Doric columns, he helped launch the mania in New Orleans for Greek Revival-style architecture. Known as the first formally trained architect in the United States,

Latrobe was born in England, and after working as a professional architect for several years in Europe, he came to the United States in 1796. Latrobe was highly influential and built a variety of private residences and public buildings, ranging from waterworks to cathedrals. He is largely responsible for the interior of the U.S. Capitol Building, and for the East Portico of the White House. He died in New Orleans of yellow fever while supervising the building of a new waterworks.

Lalaurie House

R1 **1140 Royal St** **5, 55** **To the public**

Residents of the French Quarter still tend to hurry past this otherwise delightful building because of its grim associations and reputation for ghosts. It was built in 1832 for a distinguished couple, Dr. Leonard Louis Nicolas Lalaurie and his wife, Delphine,

two socialites who were well known for their lavish and fashionable parties.

However, guests at these social events could not help but notice the condition of the servants, who were painfully thin and seemed to be terrified of Madame Lalaurie. Suspicions of maltreatment were eventually confirmed on April 10, 1834, when a fire broke out at the residence. When neighbors rushed in to extinguish the fire, they found seven half-starved and manacled slaves. A story in the local press further fueled the outrage, and a mob arrived intent on destroying the place. During the melee, Madame Lalaurie and her husband escaped unharmed. After her death in Paris in 1842, it is believed that her body was returned to New Orleans and secretly buried in St. Louis Cemetery #1 *(p112)* or #2 *(p115)*. During the Civil War, the house served as a Union headquarters; later it was used as a school, music conservatory, and gaming house.

Some locals still swear that the house, now a private residence, is haunted, and that the clanking of chains can be heard in the night.

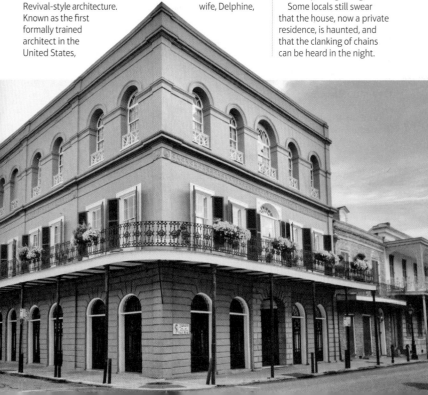

↑ Street musicians entertaining the guests at the Café du Monde, and *(inset)* a sample of the café's fare

10

Café du Monde

📍R2 🏠800 Decatur
🚊Riverfront 🚌5, 55 🕐24 hours daily 🚫Dec 25
🌐cafedumonde.com

Everyone who visits New Orleans should stop here for a plate of the famous sugar-dusted *beignets* (square donuts), accompanied by *café au lait* (or the chicory-flavored version), iced coffee, or a glass of milk. This coffeehouse, established in 1862, is perfect for relaxing at a table under the arcade and listening to the street musicians entertaining the crowds.

In the mid-19th century, as many as 500 coffeehouses operated in the French Quarter. Coffee was one of the city's most important commodities, and the coffee trade helped the to economy recover after the Civil War, when New Orleans vied with New York City to control coffee imports. During the Civil War, locals drank coffee flavored with peanuts and pecan shells, to make the supply last.

11

Gauche Villa

📍R1 🏠704 Esplanade Ave at Royal 🚊Riverfront 🚌5
🚫To the public

The beautiful cast-ironwork of Gauche Villa is uniquely integral to its overall design, which accounts for the building's harmonious appearance. Little of the ironwork in New Orleans was constructed at the same time as the building – it was usually added as an afterthought. Numerous patterns are used on the fence, the gate, the balconies, and the parapet, casting spellbinding shadows on the stucco exterior on sunny days. A bacchant surrounded by grapevines adorns the balcony, cast in Saarbrucken, Germany. Rows of anthema and other Greek floral motifs decorate the edge of the roof and the fence posts. Architect James Freret designed the house for crockery merchant John Gauche in 1856.

12

Central Grocery

📍R2 🏠923 Decatur
🚊Riverfront 🚌5
🕐9am–5pm daily
🌐centralgrocery.com

This historic store, one of the few Italian delis left in the city,

 INSIDER TIP
Sandwich Savvy

Visit Central Grocery before the lunchtime rush, as the line can sometimes stretch all the way out of the door. If you're going to try a muffuletta, buy a half portion, which is usually plenty for one person.

> The fashionable elite once paraded in their carriages past the many elegant residences on Esplanade Avenue, some of which have survived to this day.

sells all kinds of Italian food, including pasta, provolone, mozzarella, sausages, olive oil, and parmesan. In the 1890s, many Italians began to move to the French Quarter, and became major stallholders at the nearby French Market (p90). Today, customers gather at the counters at the back of the store to order another specialty, the muffuletta, a sizable sandwich filled with deli meats and cheeses. The most vital ingredient, however, is the olive salad – a blend of olives, celery, carrots, cauliflower, and capers.

Esplanade Avenue

 R1 🚌 46, 48

Today, Esplanade Avenue is the dividing line between the

Colorful historic
↓ mansions lining
Esplanade Avenue

French Quarter and Faubourg Marigny, and extends from the Mississippi to Bayou St. John. As early as the 1830s, this broad, tree-lined street cut through what was the most aristocratic Creole neighborhood of impressive villas and townhouses. The fashionable elite once paraded in their carriages past the many elegant residences on Esplanade Avenue, some of which have survived to this day. A stroll along this stretch reveals over 190 homes built before 1900. Many of these were designed by the city's foremost architects, whose styles range from Greek Revival to Italianate and Queen Anne. Most are still private residences, but some have been converted into bed-and-breakfasts. Halfway down the avenue, on the corner of Tonti Street, is Gayarré Place, named after Charles Étienne Gayarré, the historian and grandson of Étienne de Boré. At the centre, a statue of the goddess of history sits atop a terracotta monument.

STAY

Lamothe House
Step back in time in this atmospheric, 19th-century townhouse.

 R1 🏠 621 Esplanade Ave 🌐 frenchquarter guesthouses.com

$ $ $

Inn on Ursulines
One of the oldest buildings in the French Quarter - a delightful inn with a courtyard.

 R1 🏠 708 Ursulines Ave 🌐 frenchquarter guesthouses.com

$ $ $

Lafitte Guest House
The guest rooms at this Creole mansion exude period charm.

Q1 🏠 1003 Bourbon St 🌐 lafitteguest house.com

$ $ $

Lafitte's Blacksmith Shop

Q1 🏠 **941 Bourbon St**
🚌 **55, 89** ⏰ **10am-3am daily**
🌐 **lafittesblacksmith shop.com**

This is reportedly the oldest bar in New Orleans. It is an example of the French brick-between-posts (p100) style of building, and was constructed some time before 1772, although the precise date is unknown. Inside, several small fireplaces warm the place on cool evenings, and there is also a small patio containing a sculpture of Adam and Eve embracing on a bed of ivy. The sculpture was created by an artist in lieu of payment for his bar tab.

Despite its name, there is no proof that the notorious pirate brothers Jean and Pierre Lafitte operated a smithy here as a front for their smuggling activities. Very little documentation of their lives exists, so many myths have been woven around these two infamous figures. They operated as smugglers and were prominent slave traffickers, selling all manner of contraband, including seized slave ships, when the importation of slaves into the United States was forbidden in 1808. They earned local gratitude by warning the Americans of the planned British attack on New Orleans, and with their band they fought bravely in the ensuing battle. Regardless of whether this shop was indeed occupied by the Lafitte brothers, the building certainly existed to witness Jean Lafitte brazenly walking the streets when posters calling for his capture were plastered all over town.

Just up Bourbon Street from Lafitte's stands another bar, called Café Lafitte in Exile. It is so called because, until the early 1950s, the old Lafitte's was frequented by an LGBTQ+ crowd; when the bar changed hands, its new owner refused to renew the lease, and in 1953 its regular patrons were driven into exile. They established their new quarters just up the street, making Café Lafitte in Exile the oldest gay bar in the US. It is open 24 hours a day and has outdoor seating both upstairs and downstairs.

Cornstalk Fence

Q2 🏠 **915 Royal St**
🚌 **5, 55**

This handsome cast-iron landmark is one of three remaining in the city (p150). It was erected around 1850, when cast iron began replacing wrought iron (p152). Cornstalks are entwined with morning glories, and each element is painted in its natural color – yellow for the ears of corn, green for the stalks, and blue for the morning glories. A butterfly decorates the central portion of the gate, and a spray of holly adorns the bottom. It was cast by the prestigious Wood & Perot in Philadelphia.

Madame John's Legacy

Q2 🏠 **632 Dumaine St** 🚃 **Riverfront** 🚌 **5, 55**
🔒 **For refurbishments** 🌐 **lou isianastatemuseum.org**

Dating from 1789, this is one of the oldest surviving residences in the Mississippi

↑ Enjoying a drink outside Lafitte's Blacksmith Shop, the oldest bar in New Orleans

↑ A section of the intricate cast-iron Cornstalk Fence

who was born here and later served in the Venezuelan Revolutionary Navy. The galleries on the second floor are used for contemporary art exhibitions.

In 2019 Madame John's Legacy closed for refurbishments – check the website before visiting.

Valley. It is a typical Creole plantation-style house, supported on brick piers which rise some 9 ft (3m) off the ground. A veranda, accessible via French windows from all rooms, extends around the first floor.

The house's name refers to George Washington Cable's famous story *Tite Poulette* (1873), in which the hero leaves a residence as a legacy to his mistress, who sells the building, deposits the cash in a bank, and loses it all when the bank fails. Cable modeled the home in his story on this residence. In the late 19th century, the house was converted into rental apartments.

Today, exhibits in the first-floor galleries relate the history of the house and its several owner-residents. Among them were Jean Pascal, a Provençal sea captain who built the original house on this site before being killed during the Natchez revolt in 1729; and pirate-admiral René Beluche,

⑰
Washington Artillery Park and Moon Walk

☐ R2 ☐ Decatur St (between St Ann St and St Peter St) ☐ Riverfront ☐ 5, 55

Washington Artillery Park faces Jackson Square from across Decatur Street. Inside the park is an austere concrete amphi-theater with a central staircase leading to the Moon Walk. This community boardwalk was named after Mayor Maurice "Moon" Landrieu, who approved the construction of a boardwalk that made the riverfront area accessible to the public in the 1970s.

Today, Moon Walk is favored by street performers. Crowds gather to witness impromptu performances by solo artists, including guitarists, clarinetists, saxophonists, trombonists, and steel drummers, who play with an open music case at their feet to collect donations. Standing on the Moon Walk, you can enjoy a welcome break from the city's humidity, as the constant breeze along the waterfront makes the

temperature feel much cooler than in the rest of the city. It also provides an excellent vantage point from which to view the river, Jackson Square, and the surrounding area.

Stone steps lead right down from the boardwalk to the edge of the Mississippi River, where you can sit and dangle your feet in the whiskey-colored water or watch the steamboats, ocean-going barges, and other river traffic float past. Do not attempt to stand in the river, however, as the current is deceptively rapid and powerful.

If you do want to get closer to the water, there are plenty of river cruises – from quick sightseeing trips across the river on the Algiers ferry *(p129)*, to romantic night-time dinner cruises aboard the Steamboat *Natchez* accompanied by live jazz music *(p72)*.

→ A memorial Civil War cannon in Washington Artillery Park

THE ARCHITECTURE OF NEW ORLEANS

New Orleans is one of the few American cities to retain much of its historic architecture. Some French Quarter buildings date back 150 years or more, while those lining Esplanade Avenue tend to be the 19th-century former residences of the French Creole elite. The Garden District's splendid mansions are designed in a variety of period styles. It is not always easy to categorize the city's architecture, as buildings here combine multiple elements, in typical New Orleanian fashion.

FRENCH COLONIAL

Only a few buildings remain from this period, such as the Old Ursuline Convent *(p92)* and Lafitte's Blacksmith Shop *(p98)*. Most were destroyed by a series of fires: in 1788, 856 wooden buildings were destroyed; and in 1794, a further 212. However, the city's many Creole cottages reflect the style of this era. Single-storied, and featuring a pitched roof, these brightly colored residential cottages are a mix of French and Caribbean in style, popularized across the Gulf coast in the early 19th century.

↑ Laffitte's Blacksmith Shop, one of the city's few French colonial-style buildings

SPANISH COLONIAL

After the 1788 and 1794 fires, the Spanish decreed that any building of more than one story must be constructed of brick. The houses that were subsequently built can still be seen in the French Quarter. They often combine residence and store, and feature arcaded walls, heavy doors and windows, and a flagstone alleyway leading to a loggia and fountain-graced courtyard. Napoleon House, in the French Quarter, is a typical three-storied Spanish house *(p81)*.

↑ Spanish colonial-era Napoleon House, with its flat roof and heavy stone walls

← A Queen-Anne-Style raised center-hall cottage on Esplanade Avenue, and *(inset)* shotgun cottages in the French Quarter

AMERICAN TOWNHOUSE

Americans from the Atlantic states brought their own architecture with them, erecting Federal-style homes that stand out from the French or Spanish cottages. Beauregard-Keyes House is a fine example of this kind of building, with its cast iron detailing and Palladian portico *(p93)*.

RAISED CENTER-HALL COTTAGE

Most of these raised cottages feature timber eaves and an alleyway leading to a rear courtyard. The interior usually contains four symmetrical rooms separated by a center hall. The kitchen and servants' quarters are at the rear. Esplanade Avenue is lined with several kinds of these raised cottages *(p97)*.

SHOTGUN HOUSE

These were so called because a bullet fired from a shotgun through the front door would go straight through the house and out the back as all the doors were aligned. They come in single and double versions, usually with box steps in front. There are many traditional examples in Marigny *(p104)*.

THE CREOLE PLANTATION HOUSE

Refugees from Saint Domingue (Haiti) brought this style of dwelling to New Orleans. This one-story residence is usually raised on brick pillars (to catch the breezes and avoid flooding) and incorporates a wraparound veranda. Typical examples are Pitot House *(p173)*, and Laura *(p185)*.

↑ Beauregard-Keyes House, with its galleries and architraves supported by Greek Revival-style columns

↑ Laura, a Creole Plantation House, with wide verandas and a flagstone piazza

A SHORT WALK
LOWER FRENCH QUARTER

Distance 0.6 miles (0.9 km) **Time** 15 minutes
Nearest Streetcar Riverfront

The area surrounding the French Market is loaded with atmosphere, and has long been a place for meeting and mixing. First an American Indian trading post, the market developed as part of the French and then Spanish colonies. In the 19th century, it became a thriving hub of trade, thronging with international merchants and traders selling their wares, and customers meeting to drink coffee.

Today, the French Market still bustles with activity, with fresh produce, streetfood, and local souvenirs loading the many stalls. The surrounding area has plenty of bars and restaurants, and some of the oldest and most important buildings in the French Quarter.

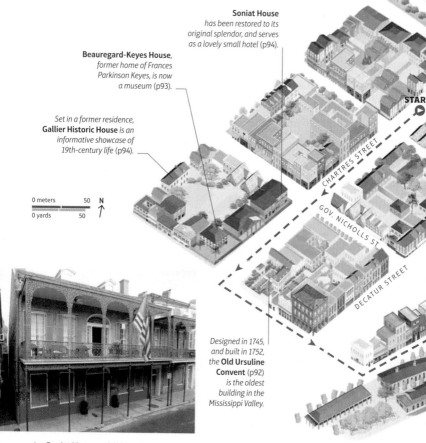

Soniat House has been restored to its original splendor, and serves as a lovely small hotel (p94).

Beauregard-Keyes House, former home of Frances Parkinson Keyes, is now a museum (p93).

Set in a former residence, **Gallier Historic House** is an informative showcase of 19th-century life (p94).

0 meters   50   N
0 yards   50

CHARTRES STREET

GOV. NICHOLLS ST

DECATUR STREET

START

Designed in 1745, and built in 1752, the **Old Ursuline Convent** (p92) is the oldest building in the Mississippi Valley.

↑ Soniat House, with its delicate ironwork balconies

↑ A restaurant counter within the busy French Market

Locator Map
For more detail see p88

LOWER
FRENCH
QUARTER

*Lower
French
Quarter*

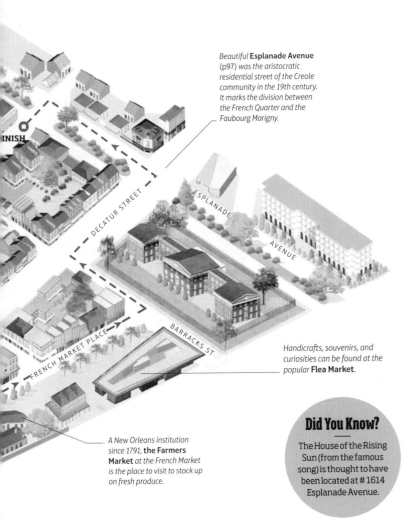

Beautiful **Esplanade Avenue**
*(p97) was the aristocratic
residential street of the Creole
community in the 19th century.
It marks the division between
the French Quarter and the
Faubourg Marigny.*

FINISH

DECATUR STREET

ESPLANADE

AVENUE

FRENCH MARKET PLACE

BARRACKS ST

*Handicrafts, souvenirs, and
curiosities can be found at the
popular* **Flea Market**.

*A New Orleans institution
since 1791,* **the Farmers
Market** *at the French Market
is the place to visit to stock up
on fresh produce.*

Did You Know?

The House of the Rising
Sun (from the famous
song) is thought to have
been located at # 1614
Esplanade Avenue.

MARIGNY, BYWATER, AND TREME

Faubourg Marigny emerged as New Orleans' first suburb in 1805, when Bernard de Marigny subdivided his family's old plantation. The small plots quickly blossomed into a vibrant working-class district, settled by French Creoles, free people of color, and German immigrants. It was once home to Jelly Roll Morton, Sidney Bechet, and other leading jazz musicians of New Orleans. The brightly painted Creole cottages and shotgun houses are now part of the Marigny historic district, and Frenchmen Street has one of the city's liveliest music scenes. An arty ambience continues into adjoining Bywater.

The area just west of the French Quarter is the Faubourg Treme, the nation's oldest African American neighborhood. Congo Square, where enslaved people gathered to make music in the 18th and 19th centuries, is hailed as the birthplace of jazz. Other landmarks include historic churches and the elaborate above-ground mausoleums in St. Louis Cemeteries #1 and #2.

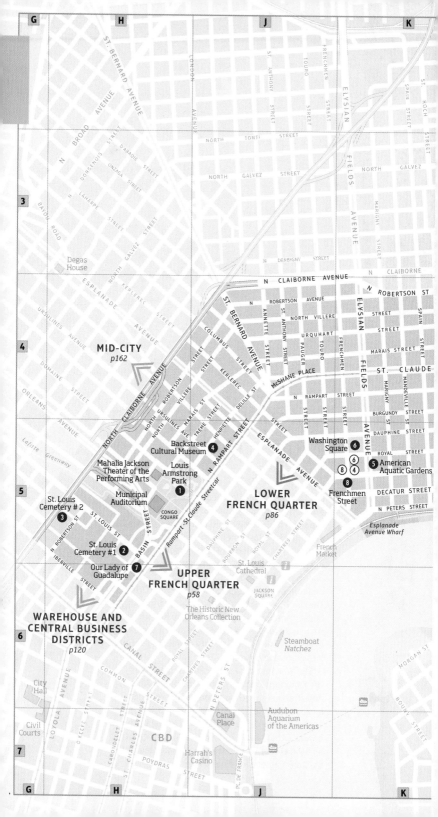

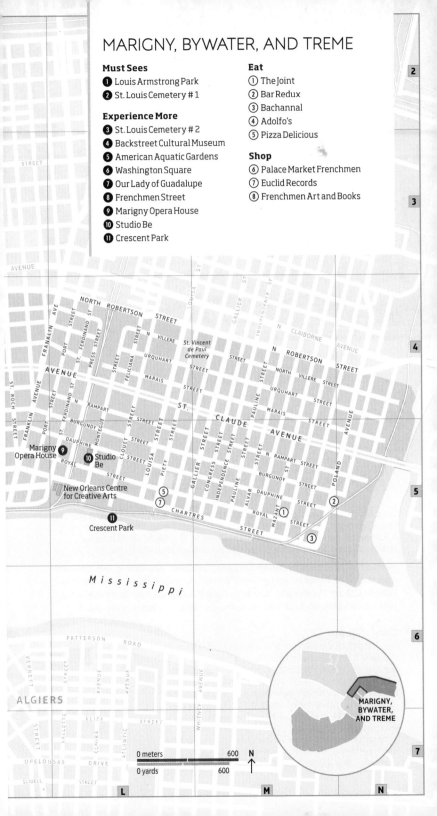

MARIGNY, BYWATER, AND TREME

Must Sees
1. Louis Armstrong Park
2. St. Louis Cemetery #1

Experience More
3. St. Louis Cemetery #2
4. Backstreet Cultural Museum
5. American Aquatic Gardens
6. Washington Square
7. Our Lady of Guadalupe
8. Frenchmen Street
9. Marigny Opera House
10. Studio Be
11. Crescent Park

Eat
1. The Joint
2. Bar Redux
3. Bachannal
4. Adolfo's
5. Pizza Delicious

Shop
6. Palace Market Frenchmen
7. Euclid Records
8. Frenchmen Art and Books

Sculpture by Steve Kline set beside the water in Louis Armstrong Park

1 ⬡ ⬡

LOUIS ARMSTRONG PARK

📍H5 🅰Louis Armstrong Park: Rampart St between St. Peter St and St. Ann St; Mahalia Jackson Theater for the Performing Arts: 1419 Basin St; Congo Square: N Rampart St between St. Peter St and St. Philip St 🚌5, 48, 88, 89 🚊Mahalia Jackson Theater for the Performing Arts: mahaliajacksontheater.com

Named for the legendary trumpeter Louis "Satchmo" Armstrong, this spacious park stands on hallowed jazz ground. Within the park, Congo Square and the Mahalia Jackson Theater play host to music festivals and concerts, while shaded paths around the artificial lake make for pleasant wandering, year round.

Congo Square

Under the Code Noir (a French edict concerning the treatment of slaves), slaveholders were forbidden to work slaves on Sunday in order to encourage them to attend church. Such minimal amounts of freedom allowed the enslaved of New Orleans to retain their African heritage, more so than those in other parts of the South. On Sunday afternoons, during the 18th and early 19th century, slaves and free people of color would gather in Congo Square, part of Armstrong Park, to meet with friends and family. They would sing, dance, and play music, performing the *calinda*, an African line dance, and the *bamboula*. These dances sowed the seeds of jazz music in New

Locator Map
For more detail see p106

LOUIS ARMSTRONG IN NEW ORLEANS

Born on August 4, 1901 in New Orleans, Armstrong spent much of his childhood singing on the streets in a quartet until he was sent to a juvenile detention home after firing a pistol in public. It was there that he learned to play the trumpet, and soon he was challenging such leading players as Joe "King" Oliver and Freddie Keppard. He left New Orleans in 1922 to join King Oliver in Chicago, and went on to build an international career, entertaining audiences until his death in 1971. Today, Elizabeth Catlett's 1976 sculpture of the legendary musician is set in Armstrong Park.

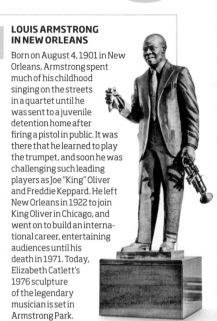

Orleans, and Congo Square is remembered as one of the birthplaces of jazz. Marie Laveau *(p115)* is said to have performed voodoo rituals here. Today, the park hosts music festivals like Essence *(p47)*, and Jazzfest *(p172)*, and Congo Square is used as venue for Mardi Gras festivities.

← Krewe du Kanaval celebrating Mardi Gras with dancing and parades in Congo Square

Mahalia Jackson Theater for the Performing Arts

This world-class theater is named for the celebrated New Orleanian gospel singer Mahalia Jackson (1911–72), who began her career singing in the local church, where her father was a pastor. Despite her strict upbringing, she fell in love with the syncopated rhythms of blues but never sang the more bawdy songs in its repertoire. Jackson was discovered in the 1930s and made her first recording in 1934. Her career took her to Carnegie Hall, the Newport Jazz Festival, and other major music venues. Jackson was active in the civil rights movement and a supporter of Martin Luther King, Jr.

The theater suffered flood damage after Hurricane Katrina but has since been restored, and today showcases broadway musicals and works of theater, along with shows by famous musicians and comedians, and dance performances.

↑ The Mahalia Jackson Theater for the Performing Arts perched on the lake

HISTORY OF NEW ORLEANS JAZZ

A modern American art form, jazz music appeared from the late 19th to early 20th century. Incorporating meandering improvisation, call and response patterns, and intricate rhythmic percussion, its roots lie in the melange of genres played in 19th-century New Orleans. Blending elements of blues, ragtime, classical music, and European brass, jazz emerged in the clubs of Storyville, and evolved in the city's parades, dances, and funerals.

CONGO SQUARE

Known as the birthplace of jazz, Congo Square is where enslaved people gathered to celebrate their one day off, playing music and dancing *(p108)*.

STORYVILLE JAZZ

Many early jazz artists were classically trained musicians, who entertained in the bordellos of Storyville *(p116)* – Buddy Bolden, King Oliver, Jelly Roll Morton, Sidney Bechet, and Freddie Keppard among them.

RIVERBOAT JAZZ BANDS

After Storyville was closed in 1917, many of New Orleans' best musicians moved to perform on the city's riverboats like Steamboat *Natchez (p74)*.

STREETS OF JAZZ

Many jazz greats, Armstrong included *(p109)*, started out playing on the streets. This tradition continues, with bands playing on every corner, and Second Lines marching the neighborhoods *(p114)*.

↑ New Orleans-born jazz legend Louis Armstrong performing in 1968

→
Sidney Bechet performs with Jelly Roll Morton's New Orleans Jazzmen in 1939

Local Legends

Sidney Bechet (1897–1959)

▽ Solo clarinetist and saxophonist, and composer, Bechet toured the world. He moved to Paris in 1950.

Danny Barker (1909–1994)

▽ Played guitar and banjo with the big bands in 1930s and 1940s New York City before returning to New Orleans.

Jelly Roll Morton (1890–1941)

△ A pianist and one of the first great jazz composers, Jelly Roll Morton began his career in Storyville.

Lil Hardin (1898–1971)

△ Pianist, composer, and singer who collaborated with (and married) Louis Armstrong.

Boswell Sisters (1925–36)

▽ A trio of of singers whose up-tempo tunes propelled them to national radio in the 1930s.

Louise "Blue Lu" Barker (1913–98)

△ A jazz and blues singer, said to have influenced famous stars like Billie Holiday and Eartha Kitt.

Blanche Thomas (1922–77)

A favorite in the bars along Bourbon Street, Thomas sang the blues with artists like Al Hirt.

Terence Blanchard (1962-)

△ A trumpeter and composer, famous for scoring and playing the music for the films of director Spike Lee.

ST. LOUIS CEMETERY #1

⚑ H5 **⌂ Basin St between St. Louis and Conti** **☎ 482-5065**
🚌 48, 46, 52, 57 **🕐 9am–3pm Mon–Sat, 9am–noon Sun**

Spanning one square block, St. Louis Cemetery #1 is the final resting place for many thousands. Its narrow alleyways lined with elaborately carved mausoleums make for a fascinating wander.

This cemetery opened in 1789 and is the oldest in the city. By 1829, St. Louis #1 was already filled, mostly with victims of yellow fever. Although Catholic, at one time the cemetery accepted Protestants (these graves were later moved). The narrow alleyways are full of mausoleums, many in advanced stages of decay. In New Orleans, people are usually buried above ground rather than below, because the city sits below sea level, and therefore deep digging is not allowed in many areas.

Numerous legendary local figures are buried here in impressive crypts. The largest tomb belongs to the Société Française de Bienfaisance, which contains an overwhelming 70 vaults. The tallest monument, sculpted by Pietro Gualdi in 1857 for $40,000, belongs to the Italian Society.

> 💬 INSIDER TIP
> **Take a Tour**
>
> Under rules set by the Archdiocese of New Orleans, all visitors to St. Louis Cemetery #1 must be accompanied by a licensed tour guide. Guided tours by Save Our Cemeteries (*saveourcemeteries.org*) and Two Chicks (*twochicks walkingtours.com*) provide excellent local information.

St. Louis Cemetery #1's maze of tombs, and *(inset)* exploring on a guided tour ↑

↑ Nicholas Cage's mausoleum,
where the actor plans to be interred

↑ Paying respects at the
tomb of Marie Laveau

Henry Latrobe

A plaque memorializes Benjamin Henry Latrobe (1764–1820), an architect who came to New Orleans to build a waterworks. He died in 1820 of yellow fever. No one knows where his remains are. In 1823 many bodies were moved from St. Louis Cemetery #1 to Lafayette Cemetery and then Metairie Cemetery in the 1950s. Somehow, Latrobe's body got lost in the shuffle.

Jean Etienne Boré

The plantation owner who was the city's first post-colonial mayor is buried in a low brick vault. Boré (1741–1820) contributed much to the city's prosperity as he was the first to granulate sugar on a commercial scale in 1796.

Bernard de Marigny

▷ A French-Creole aristocrat, Marigny (1788–1871) is known for having introduced craps (dice) to the United States. At age 15, he inherited the sum of $7 million, but quickly gambled the money away.

Marie Laveau

◁ The most famous mausoleum belongs to Marie Laveau (1801–1881). Crowds visit her tomb (though some believe it is not the correct one) to leave unusual voodoo "gifts," or mark it with an "X," which symbolizes a request that she grant a particular wish.

Homer Adolph Plessy

A free person of color, Plessy (1862–1925) challenged the Separate Car Act segregation law, and was tried in the Plessy v. Ferguson U.S. Supreme Court case in the 1890s.

Ernest Nathan Morial

▷ A leading civil rights advocate, Ernest "Dutch" Morial (1929–1989) was the first African American mayor of New Orleans. Morial served from 1978 to 1986, contributing to the city's urban development. His son, Marc Morial, would also serve as mayor.

EXPERIENCE MORE

3

St. Louis Cemetery #2

◉ H3 Ⓐ Iberville to St Louis St, between N Claiborne Ave and N Robertson St ☎ 482-5065 🚌 48, 46, 52, 57 🕐 9am–3pm Mon–Sat, 9am–noon Sun

By the end of the colonial period, and mostly because of a devastating series of cholera and yellow fever epidemics (p51), this cemetery was established as the natural extension of St. Louis Cemetery #1 (p112) around 1823. The final resting place for much of New Orleans' 19th-century Creole aristocracy, it contains remarkably ornate mausoleums. Many of them were designed by Jacques Nicholas Bussière de Pouilly, who arrived in New Orleans from France in the 1830s. His plans were inspired by the tombs in Paris's Père Lachaise Cemetery. Grand in design and scale, and modeled on Greek, Egyptian, and other Classical styles, the patterns for these ambitious mausoleums became very popular in New Orleans. The tombs are like impressive residences, often enclosed within beautiful wrought-iron gates, featuring elaborate motifs such as lyres, winged hourglasses, hearts, and urns with arrows. The fences around the tombs are some of the finest wrought ironwork in the city. Unique intricate immortelles made of wire, beads, and glass represent everlasting tributes to the dead. Among the notables buried here are General Jean Baptiste Plauché, who fought with Andrew Jackson at the Battle of New Orleans (p50).

> 💬 INSIDER TIP
> ### Take a Second Look
>
> Second Line parades trace back to the jazz funeral, when mourners and a brass band would be followed by a "second line" of revellers. Today, these exhuberant parades, organized by the city's Social Aid and Pleasure Clubs, enliven the Treme neighborhood most Sundays. Stop and watch (or even join in) as the celebrations unfold.

↑ A wide avenue of St. Louis Cemetery #2, and (inset) the elaborate Joseph Barelli tomb

→

Mardi Gras celebrations outside the Backstreet Cultural Museum

> **The tombs are like impressive residences, often enclosed within beautiful wrought-iron gates, featuring elaborate motifs.**

J. N. B. de Pouilly himself is buried in a modest wall vault with his brother, who was also an architect. Other famous New Orleans figures buried here include jazz musician Danny Barker, and pirate Dominique You, who rests in the main aisle in a tomb marked with a Masonic emblem and the inscription: "This New Bayard could have witnessed the end of the world without fear or trembling."

Near the cemetery office, the Barelli tomb recalls the tragedy of November 15, 1849, when the steamer *Louisiana* exploded, killing 86 people, including the young son of Joseph Barelli, who erected the memorial in 1856. Five sculpted angels hover around the tomb and a bas relief depicts the explosion.

A common legend says that Napoleon Bonaparte's followers were waiting for his arrival in New Orleans from his exile in St. Helena, but since he died beforehand on December 20, 1821, a funeral service for him was held in the cemetery. Guided tours, led by several organizations *(p112)*, will help visitors get the most out of their time at this fascinating site.

4

Backstreet Cultural Museum

📍J5 🏠1116 Henriette Delille Street 🚋St. Claude at Pauger 🚌Ursulines Avenue ⏰10am-4pm Mon-Fri, 10am-3pm Sat 🌐backstreetmuseum.org

What could be mistaken for a residential home offers a rare chance to peek into one of the city's more secretive cultural groups: the Mardi Gras Indians *(p66)*. African and American Indian influences are at play in the costumes and traditions of these colorful Mardi Gras groups, who parade in elaborate feathered and sequined masks and costumes each year. Seeing the outfits up close on display at this small museum, you can appreciate the painstaking detail that goes into every rhinestone on these handmade wonders. The museum also has information and artifacts relating to the city's unique traditions of jazz funerals, second lines, and Social Aid and Pleasure Clubs.

> **VODOU WORSHIP**
>
> Vodou (or voodoo as it is commonly known today) arrived in New Orleans from Africa, via the Caribbean, where it originated as a form of ancestor worship among the West African peoples who were brought to North America as slaves. With the revolution in Saint Domingue in 1793, slaves and free people of color arrived as refugees and increased the practice in the city. The most famous of all 19th-century vodou leaders was Marie Laveau (c. 1794–1881). Mythologized as the "voodoo queen," it is thought that she used Catholic elements like prayer, incense, and saints in her rituals, which she opened to the public for an admission fee. Laveau is reputed to have held celebrations along the Bayou St. John on St. John's Eve, a festival observed by the Catholic calendar. She is buried at St. Louis Cemetery #1 *(p112)*.

⑤

American Aquatic Gardens

📍 K5 🏠 621 Elysian Fields 🚌 5, 55 🕐 9am- 4pm daily 🚫 Public hols 🌐 american aquaticgardens.com

This delightful locally owned "store," which occupies half a city block, is the largest – and widely considered the best – aquatic plant nursery and garden supply store in the United States. The tropical climate in New Orleans is the perfect environment for aquatic and exotic plantlife, and the American Aquatic Gardens are worth a visit just for the glorious displays in the outdoor gardens, including an inviting Asian garden complete with decorative Buddhas and lanterns. The water gardens contain an exquisite array of water lilies (some varieties of which are bred exclusively in-house), as well as spectacular sculpted fountains, handsome statuary, attractive pond designs, and ornamental ceramic pots and wall planters.

⑥

Washington Square

📍 K5 🏠 Frenchmen between Royal and Dauphine 🕐 9am-6pm daily 🚌 5, 55

Washington Square, one of the earliest parks to be laid out in New Orleans, was created in 1808, and named after the Washington 141st Field Artillery Regiment in 1838. It lies at the center of the Faubourg Marigny on Elysian Fields, and is a good place to throw a frisbee and for ball games, or just to relax on the green areas it offers. There are also open-air concerts and plays here in summer and caroling in December.

---

⑦

Our Lady of Guadalupe

📍 H6 🏠 411 N Rampart St 🚌 48, 46, 52, 57 🕐 9am-5pm Mon- Sat 🌐 judes hrine.com

Originally consecrated as the Mortuary Chapel of St.

Anthony, this chapel was built on the outskirts of the French Quarter in 1826, when funerals were no longer being held in St. Louis Cathedral for fear of spreading yellow fever (p51). After the service, bodies were taken directly from the chapel to St. Louis Cemetery #1 (p112). In 1918, it was renamed and put under the administration of the Missionary Oblates of Mary Immaculate.

The church is distinguished by several brilliantly colored stained-glass windows, each representing a different saint honored by devoted New Orleanians. The most visited altar is dedicated to St. Jude, known as the "patron saint of hopeless causes," but a more

STORYVILLE

From 1897 to 1917, the 38 blocks bounded by Iberville, Basin, Robertson, and St. Louis were set aside as a legal red-light district by alderman Sidney Story. Saloons and brothels lined Basin Street, and bawdy houses clustered along Dauphine, St. Louis, Conti, and Bienville. At No. 317 Basin Street, Countess Willie Piazza held court, and regularly employed pianist Jelly Roll Morton. The district was officially closed in 1917 by the Navy Department. In the 1930s, the Federal government leveled Storyville to make way for low-income housing. As such, little remains of Storyville today, but it has inspired many works of fiction, including the 1978 movie *Pretty Baby* (below).

Did You Know?

In the early 1900s, prostitutes were listed in the "Blue Book," available at bars all over Storyville.

↑ Colorful lights and palm trees brightening up Frenchmen Street

light-hearted one stands to the left of the exit; this is dedicated to New Orleans' very own St. Expedite, whose name is not in any official dictionary of saints. According to legend, a crate marked with the word *spedito!* ("rush!") arrived in the chapel one day. The statue inside it was removed and mounted on the wall, and its name was confused with the word on the box. To this day, locals visit the altar to pray for help when they need something in a hurry. St. Expedite is also associated with voodoo, which is why the church is sometimes referred to as the "Voodoo Church." Our Lady of Guadalupe is the official place of worship for the police and fire departments, whose altar stands to the right of the main altar.

8

Frenchmen Street

K5 Elysian Fields

Named after a group of French rebels executed under Spanish rule, the Marigny section of this street has traditionally been a local's secret. More visitors are now coming here, drawn by the mix of music, lively bars, and restaurants, and the nightly art market. Every evening, live jazz bands strike up in various venues, including famous clubs such as the swinging **Spotted Cat** (one of the city's oldest jazz clubs), intimate **Blue Nile**, and jazz bistro **Snug Harbor**. There is often a one-drink minimum, but you'll be rewarded with impeccable live traditional jazz and, if you're lucky, some swing dancing by talented locals.

Brass bands entertain on the corner of Frenchmen and Chartres, and street poets and artists line the pavements. At Palace Market Frenchmen, which opens in the evening until late, visitors can browse the eclectic stalls filled with works by local artists, cocktail in hand. Several late-night dining options are available, most notably **Three Muses**, where you can enjoy tapas with live music and cocktails.

SHOP

Palace Market Frenchmen

An atmospheric nightly market where the city's most innovative artists sell their work. Vibrant visual arts, handicrafts and clothing are all on sale.

K5
619 Frenchmen St
palacemarketnola.com

Euclid Records

One of the city's oldest and best indie music stores, this record store is a treasure trove of all genres, and the staff are well informed and especially helpful.

L5 3301 Chartres St
euclidnola.com

Frenchmen Art and Books

A Frenchmen Street institution and one of the few remaining indie bookstores in the city. New and used editions abound, and there is a wonderful selection of art prints.

K5
600 Frenchmen St
frenchmenart andbooks.com

The Spotted Cat
623 Frenchmen St
spottedcatmusicclub.com

Blue Nile
532 Frenchmen St
bluenilelive.com

Snug Harbor
626 Frenchmen St
snugjazz.com

Three Muses
536 Frenchmen St
3musesnola.com

EAT

The Joint

Fans of this BBQ joint's home-smoked ribs, brisket, and pulled pork pack the place out daily.

📍M5 🏠701 Mazant St
🌐alwayssmokin.com

$$ⓈⓈⓈ$$

Bar Redux

On the outskirts of the Bywater, this charming dive has a surprisingly good kitchen and a varied program of music and comedy.

📍M5 🏠801 Poland Ave
📞504-592-7083

$$ⓈⓈⓈ$$

Bachannal

Pick up a bottle and a cheese plate and enjoy the live jazz at this expanded venue with an inviting backyard.

📍M5 🏠600 Poland Ave
🌐bachanallwine.com

$$ⓈⓈⓈ$$

Adolfo's

Climb the rickety stairs to this cozy Italian restaurant for an evocative ambience and delicious home-made dishes.

📍K5 🏠611 Frenchmen St 📞948-3800

$$ⓈⓈⓈ$$

Pizza Delicious

With its unusual daily specials and good vegetarian and vegan offerings, this kitchen makes some of the best pizza in town.

📍L5 🏠617 Piety St
🌐pizzadelicious.com

$$ⓈⓈⓈ$$

→

The Rusty Rainbow bridge at Crescent Park with the downtown skyline beyond

 ⑨

Marigny Opera House

📍L5 🏠725 St Ferdinand St ⏰For performances 🌐marignyoperahouse.org

Many New Orleans venues are former churches, but none is quite as impressive as this self-proclaimed "church of the arts." The building itself, dating back to 1853, was originally the Holy Trinity Catholic Church, serving the German Catholic community of the Marigny. Architect Theodore Giraud designed the church using elements of the Romanesque and Baroque styles, and the building is dominated by its elegant twin bell towers with onion-shaped domes. In 2011 this historic landmark was transformed into a venue for classical music, dance, and theater. The opera house now has an impressive program of operatic productions and contemporary dance, and is home to the award-winning Marigny Opera Ballet company, which produces original pieces to live musical accompaniment. The venue has also become a popular venue for weddings, including those of famous musicians such as singer Solange Knowles and Patrick Carney of the Black Keys.

---

⑩

Studio Be

📍L5 🏠2941 Royal St
🚇Elysian Fields ⏰Wed-Sat 2-8pm 🌐bmike.com/project/studio-be

This huge studio warehouse is dedicated to showcasing the work of New Orleans–based visual artist Brandon Odums (also known as BMike), who specializes in striking, colorful, large-scale murals and paintings illustrating scenes from African American culture in the city and black cultural leaders and icons. After a stint as a music video director for hip hop luminaries such as Curren$y, Juvenile, and Yasiin Bey (Mos Def), Odums began to experiment with the

medium of graffiti, founding guerilla art hubs in dilapidated housing developments. He is now one of the most in-demand street artists in the world.

The varied exhibits on show at Studio Be show off the whole range of Odum's talent, with mixed-media pieces including sculpture and video. For most people, though, the real stars of the show, and the works for which he is most famous, are the incredible floor-to-ceiling portraits. The gallery is an inspiring example of successful community art and a welcome contrast to the more conventional tastes of the Uptown art galleries.

> **Bike paths, dog runs, and picnic areas with great views of the city skyline were built, and the area was given a brand new lease of life as Crescent Park.**

New Orleans' art scene will reward visitors willing to explore beyond the mass-produced paintings of jazz musicians and gaudy landscapes of the French Quarter, and this warehouse gallery is well worth anyone's time.

Crescent Park

◎ L5 ⬠ Crescent Park Trail, Mississippi Riverside ⊞ Elysian Fields ◯ 6am–7.30pm daily ⓦ crescentparknola.org

A few years ago, the banks of the Mississippi River along the Marigny and Bywater neighborhoods were an unsightly, disused stretch of industrial wasteland, and the nearby residents had no access to the riverside. In 2015, as part of the post–Hurricane Katrina revitalization project, this all changed, and the riverside was redeveloped into a mile and a half of linear green spaces for public use. Bike

paths, dog runs, and picnic areas with great views of the downtown city skyline were built, and the area was given a brand new lease of life as Crescent Park. Some of the industrial spaces have been preserved and repurposed as event facilities for concerts, weddings, and parties.

The most famous element of the park is the Rusty Rainbow, a striking, curved iron walkway that reaches across the train tracks. Stroll the length of the park for a scenic route from the Bywater into the Marigny and the French Quarter.

 PICTURE PERFECT
Pretty Crescent City

Crescent Park follows the gentle bend of the Mississippi - make your way down to the park's riverside at the Marigny end to snap an extraordinary panorama of the city's skyline.

WAREHOUSE AND CENTRAL BUSINESS DISTRICTS

When the Americans arrived in New Orleans following the Louisiana Purchase of 1803, they developed a community on the upriver side of Canal Street, in Faubourg Ste. Marie. Separated from the Creole French Quarter by a median of "neutral ground" along the center of Canal Street, this neighborhood was known as the American Sector. As global trade from the port of New Orleans flourished, a commercial and residential district grew behind the waterfront. The Central Business District, or CBD, is still the city's commercial hub, its narrow streets lined with Victorian warehouses, banks, and offices. The 1970s saw a wave of demolitions along the riverfront as historic buildings began to crumble, and modern skyscrapers rose along Poydras Street, along with the enormous Superdome.

Southwest from Poydras Street, is the Warehouse District, where 19th-century brick buildings once housed goods at the busy port in the days before containerized shipping. Following a steady period of decline in the 20th century, the 1984 World's Fair transformed this semi-dilapidated neighborhood. Today, the Ogden Museum of Southern Art and vibrant clusters of galleries and theaters lend this quarter its nickname: the Arts District.

WAREHOUSE AND CENTRAL BUSINESS DISTRICTS

Must Sees
1. Audubon Aquarium of the Americas
2. The National WWII Museum

Experience More
3. Ferry to Algiers
4. Woldenberg Riverfront Park
5. Outlet Collection at Riverwalk
6. Spanish Plaza
7. St. Patrick's Church
8. World Trade Center
9. Canal Place
10. Harrah's Casino
11. Audubon Butterfly Garden and Insectarium
12. Gallier Hall
13. Mercedes-Benz Superdome
14. Saenger Theatre
15. Confederate Memorial Hall
16. New Orleans Contemporary Arts Center
17. Ogden Museum of Southern Art

Eat
1. Cochon Restaurant
2. Compère Lapin
3. Domenica
4. Emeril's New Orleans

Drink
5. The Little Gem Saloon
6. The Sazerac Bar
7. W.I.N.O

Stay
8. Le Pavillon
9. The Old 77 Hotel and Chandlery
10. The Eliza Jane
11. The Roosevelt Hotel

Shop
12. Meyer the Hatter

① ⚡ Ⓜ 💻 🛍

AUDUBON AQUARIUM OF THE AMERICAS

📍J7 🏛Canal Street at Mississippi River 🚌5, 55, 57 🕙10am–5pm daily 🚫Dec 24 and 25, Thanksgiving, Mardi Gras 🌐audubonnatureinstitute.org/aquarium

Rated one of the best in the country, the Audubon Aquarium is a multi-sensory attraction. Dive into a kaleidoscope of fascinating underwater worlds, and observe myriad exotic and endangered sea creatures in mesmerizing natural habitats.

The collection at the Audubon Aquarium of the Americas spans the underwater world, from the Caribbean and the Amazon Rainforest, to the waters that give New Orleans its lifeblood – the Mississippi River and the Gulf of Mexico. Highlights include the Great Maya Reef, where visitors walk through a clear tunnel and feel as if immersed in a submerged Mayan city. In the Amazon Rainforest, piranhas lurk in the waters that flow under a forest canopy alive with tropical birds, wild orchids, and an anaconda. Around 500 different species make up the collection – many of which live in the Gulf of Mexico exhibit, the aquarium's largest tank. This impressive exhibit is also home to a quarter-scale replica of an offshore oil rig.

> 💬 INSIDER TIP
> **Movie Magic**
>
> Need a break? Catch a film (included in the entry price) at the Entergy Giant Screen Theater. Its cutting-edge projection and sound systems bring the natural world to life.

TOP 5 AQUARIUM CREATURES

White Alligator
The blue-eyed white alligator from Louisiana is one of the world's rarest 'gators.

Seahorses
Beautiful seahorses and sea dragons look like legendary sea monsters in miniature.

Sea Otters
Two rescued Southern sea otters (an endangered species) make a playful pair.

Jellyfish
Ethereal jellies float in the Jelly Gallery's cornerless tanks known as "Kriesels."

Penguins
Many of the delightful African penguins in the penguin colony were born at the aquarium.

Did You Know?

The vast Gulf of Mexico tank holds 400,000 gallons (150,000 liters) of water.

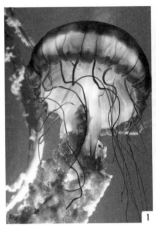

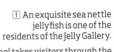

1 An exquisite sea nettle jellyfish is one of the residents of the Jelly Gallery.

2 A tunnel takes visitors through the breathtaking Great Maya Reef exhibit.

3 The entrance leads to two floors of world-class tanks, pools, and interactive exhibits.

↑ The Gulf of Mexico tank, featuring a wealth of fish and other sealife

② ⬠ Ⓜ ⬚ 🖐

THE NATIONAL WWII MUSEUM

📍 H8 🏛 945 Magazine Street and Howard Avenue 🚍 11, 41
🕐 9am–5pm daily 🚫 Thanksgiving, Dec 24 and 25, Mardi Gras
🌐 nationalww2museum.org

Originally founded in 2000 as the National D-Day Museum, this hugely impressive archive is a magnificent memorial to the U.S. servicemen and women who helped secure the Allied victory in World War II.

This museum honors the veterans of World War II and the role played by the U.S. military in the conflict. There's also a local connection in the form of New Orleans shipbuilder Andrew Higgins, whose company built many of the U.S. landing craft used in the war. The Home Front, the European and Pacific Theaters, and the D-Day Invasion are the museum's principal exhibits, combining everything from news reports to interactive personal stories to some of the era's vehicles and weapons. Exhibits include the immersive, hands-on submarine exhibit – Final Mission: USS Tang Submarine Experience – and a poignant 4D movie presentation, Beyond All Boundaries; this multimedia epic is presented in the state-of-the-art Solomon Victory Theater and narrated by Tom Hanks. The museum is undergoing a huge $400 million expansion that will result in new exhibits, expanded public spaces, and a dedicated hotel. The projects are estimated to be completed by 2021.

← The Campaigns of Courage pavilion, covering the European and Pacific theaters of war

→ A World War II German motorcycle from the museum's collection

THE HIGGINS BOAT

Louisiana was the home of Higgins Industries, which manufactured a revolutionary amphibious landing craft - The Higgins Boat. Trialed in the state's renowned swamps and marshes, the craft was perfectly suited for testing wartime conditions. Around 20,000 were deployed during World War II.

Did You Know?

The museum has its own female vocal trio, the Victory Belles, who sing wartime-era songs.

←
Iconic aircraft, tanks, and trucks in the U.S. Freedom Pavilion: the Boeing Center

EXPERIENCE MORE

❸
Ferry to Algiers

📍 J7 🚏 Pier is at the end of Canal St 🚊 Riverfront 🚌 55, 57 🌐 norta.com

From the foot of Canal Street, a ferry will take you over the Mississippi to the historic neighborhood of Algiers on the West Bank *(p207)*. Algiers was established in 1719 and is the second oldest part of the city. For over a century, it was used as a holding area for imported slaves, who were held here before being sold on. The area was not connected directly to the rest of the city until a bridge was built in the late 1950s, so it has a distinct, small-town feel. It is packed with beautiful late-Victorian churches, homes, parks, and businesses, and at its heart is the Romanesque Revival–style Algiers Courthouse, dating from 1896, which is visible from the French Quarter across the river. It continues to serve as a courthouse for the residents of the entire city, and is home to various municipal offices.

At the beginning of the 20th century, Algiers was home to many of the early jazz artists, such as Red Allen, Jimmy Palao, and Kid Thomas Valentine. Today, the Algiers courthouse is the setting for much of the **Old Algiers RiverFest**, a weekend-long festival celebrating the role of the area in the development of jazz. Visitors can enjoy great live music and various arts and crafts, and sample typical New Orleans cuisine. The festival takes place in April each year.

Old Algiers RiverFest
🌐 oldalgiersmainstreet.com

---

❹
Woldenberg Riverfront Park

📍 J6 🚏 2 Canal St 🚊 Riverfront 🚌 3, 55, 57 🕐 Dawn – dusk daily

The 16-acre Woldenberg Park extends all the way along the riverfront from St. Peter Street up to the Outlet Collection at Riverwalk, providing an outstanding garden setting studded with

 GREAT VIEW
Mississippi Magic

The Algiers ferry can be caught from just behind Harrah's Casino. A few minutes after the ferry leaves the pier, you'll be rewarded with one of the best views of the city skyline anywhere.

↑ The city skyline seen from the Canal Street ferry at dusk

contemporary sculptures. The park is named for Malcolm Woldenberg, a local businessman and philanthropist, who helped to build it. From Jackson Square, visitors can access the riverfront park via Washington Artillery Park and Moon Walk. Here, many of the city's street performers can be found. Moon walk is named after Moon Landrieu, widely regarded as paving the way for the first black mayor, "Dutch" Morial, to be elected in 1978 (p53).

⑤ Outlet Collection at Riverwalk

📍 J7 🏠 1 Poydras St
🚋 Riverfront 🚌 3, 55, 57, 65
🕐 10am–9pm Mon–Sat, 10am–7pm Sun 🌐 riverwalkneworleans.com

This huge riverside shopping mall, designed by the same company that developed Boston's Faneuil Hall, contains more than 140 stores, including brand-name favorites like Ann Taylor, Brookstone, Nine West, and Gap. The entire top floor

←

A bronze Malcolm Woldenberg and young companion at Woldenberg Riverfront Park

houses a food court, selling a variety of cuisines, while a highlight of the ground floor is Creole Delicacies Gourmet Shop, which offers a two-hour cookery course.

In addition to shopping opportunities, the mall has an outdoor walkway that runs along the Mississippi, giving visitors one of the best views of the river and its traffic in the city. International and other cruise ships dock alongside the marketplace, the most notable being those operated by the Delta Queen Steamboat Company, established in 1890. A number of information plaques attached to railings along the walkway describe everything from the types of boats plying their trade on the river to the seagulls that drift up from the Gulf of Mexico.

Spanish Plaza

📍 J7 🏠 2 Canal St
🚋 Riverfront 🚌 3, 55, 57

This small plaza, situated at the entrance to the Outlet Collection at Riverwalk, is a good place to take a rest and enjoy an uninterrupted view of the river. A fountain stands at its center, surrounded by a circular mosaic bench on which the coats of arms of Spain are depicted.

The Creole Queen paddle-wheeler departs from the plaza and takes passengers downriver to the Chalmette Battlefield Park, the site of Andrew Jackson's victory at the Battle of New Orleans during the Civil War. Rangers provide a 40-minute tour of the site. Adjacent to the battlefield is Chalmette National Cemetery, where thousands of Union soldiers are buried. An antebellum house, the Malus-Beauregard home, stands on park property. This residence was built in 1833 and purchased in 1880 by the son of confederate General P. G. T. Beauregard.

EAT

Cochon Restaurant
This rustic-looking dining room is a celebration of all things porcine, with meats prepared on the premises to the exacting standards of the in-house recipes.
📍 J8
🏠 930 Tchoupitoulas St
🌐 cochonrestaurant.com
$$$

Compère Lapin
Cool, sophisticated restaurant serving Caribbean food, bringing innovative twists to St. Lucian and Creole classics.
📍 H7
🏠 535 Tchoupitoulas St
🌐 comperelapin.com
$$$

Domenica
One of the best downtown Italian restaurants. Its daily happy hour (2–6pm) is particularly good, with many of the speciality pizzas and wines by the glass sold at half price.
📍 H6 🏠 123 Baronne St
🌐 domenicarestaurant.com
$$$

Emeril's New Orleans
The flagship joint of the city's most famous chef, Emeril Lagasse, where the classy New Orleans classic dishes stand up to his reputation.
📍 J8
🏠 800 Tchoupitoulas St
🌐 emerilsrestaurants.com
$$$

7

St. Patrick's Church

H7 **724 Camp St**
St Charles **11, 41**
9am–4pm Mon-Fri
oldstpatricks.org

Old St. Patrick's Church was completed in 1841 to minister to the Irish Catholic population at the urging of Father James Ignatius Mullon. The brothers Charles and James Dakin were the original architects, but James Gallier, Sr., the mastermind behind Gallier Hall (p132), replaced them. St. Patrick's is an impressive architectural feat, with a 185-ft- (60-m-) high tower, a Gothic-inspired interior, and splendid stained-glass vaulting in the sanctuary.

Behind the altar are three paintings by the French artist Leon Pomarede. At the center is a copy of Raphael's *The Transfiguration*, flanked by *St. Patrick Baptizing the Irish Princesses* and *Christ Walking on Water*. Each of these works

dates to 1841. Although the Irish community has largely moved away from the area, the congregation still draws loyal followers from other districts. Father Mullon is still remembered as an ardent Confederate. He prayed publicly for a Confederate victory, and when General Benjamin "Beast" Butler (p50) accused him of refusing to bury a Union soldier, he volunteered that he would be "very happy to bury them all." At noon on St. Patrick's Day, a mass is attended by most Catholics as an important part of the festivities held all over the city.

8

World Trade Center

J7 **2 Canal St**
Riverfront **57, 65**
wtcno.org

The World Trade Center was designed by Edward Durrell Stone in the 1960s. Originally

The grand tower of St. Patrick's Church rising into a clear azure sky ↑

SHOP

Meyer the Hatter
Hats are de rigueur at almost every occasion in New Orleans, so why not treat yourself to a well-made classic from this independent hat-maker – the largest in the South – that has been here since 1894.

H6 **120**
St. Charles Ave
Sun **meyer thehatter.com**

called the International Trade Mart Building, it housed the headquarters of various mercantile companies and consulates. Architecturally, it has little to recommend it; however, being built in the shape of a Greek cross, it serves as a useful landmark.

Currently, the building is mostly vacant. The City of New Orleans, as its owner, is exploring ways to redevelop the building to take advantage of its prime location at the foot of Canal Street.

9

Canal Place

J7 **Canal St and N Peters St** **Canal** **5**
10am-7pm Mon-Fri, 10am-8pm Sat, noon-7pm Sun **canalplacestyle.com**

Downtown's most upscale shopping mall is anchored by Saks Fifth Avenue, and contains stores such as Brooks Brothers, Williams-Sonoma, Banana Republic, Anthropologie, and Coach. The third floor features the food court, plus the only downtown cinema that shows foreign and arthouse films.

The mall also houses the Cinebarre Canal Place, an upscale cinema that offers

the latest blockbuster films and the option to dine while watching. There are spectacular views of the Mississippi from the fourth floor.

Harrah's Casino

📍 J7 🏠 228 Poydras St
🚋 Riverfront 🚌 3, 57, 65
🕐 24 hrs daily 🌐 harrahs neworleans.com

This casino is close to the riverfront, just a block away from the Mississippi River. It is the only land-based casino offering table games in the state. Harrah's also offers a vast ballroom in addition to a wide range of games.

Masquerade is a state-of-the-art entertainment venue set at the heart of the casino. It features a four-story tower surrounded by a stage for the free nightly shows starring

↑ Touring the Audubon Insectarium, and *(inset)* two of the Butterfly Garden's residents

some of the nation's top DJs. There is also an ice-topped bar and exclusive VIP lounge area.

Audubon Butterfly Garden & Insectarium

📍 J6 🏠 423 Canal St
🚋 Canal 🚌 5 🕐 10am–4:30pm Tue–Sun
🌐 auduboninstitute.org/visit/insectarium

This state-of-the-art museum, is located within the U.S. Customs House, an architectural landmark originally designed by Alexander Thompson Wood. Construction of the Custom House began in 1847 and was

completed in 1881. Inside, the main Marble Hall is a dramatic space under a ground-glass ceiling with a decorative stained-glass border and a skylight above. Over the years, the building has served as a post office, armory, and prison.

Today, this outpost of the Audubon Nature Institute is home to fascinating interactive displays of termites, butterflies, beetles, and roaches. Highlights are the cookery show, which illustrates the art of cooking with insects, and Metamorphosis, a lab where visitors can observe insect courtship and life cycles. There are also giant animatronic bugs and a gift shop with insect-themed products. Visitors can also sample critter-related cuisine at the Bug Appetit café.

> **Highlights are the cookery show, which illustrates the art of cooking with insects, and Metamorphosis, a lab where visitors can observe insect courtship and life cycles.**

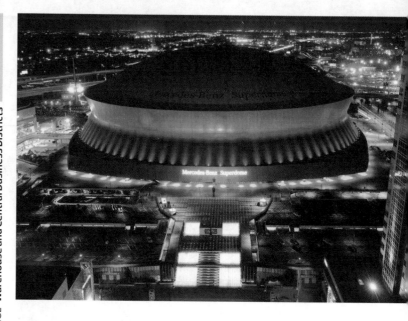

⑫
Gallier Hall

📍 H7 ⌖ 545 St Charles Ave 🚋 St Charles ⏱ For tours only, check website 🌐 nola.gov/gallier-hall

James Gallier, Sr.'s Greek Revival masterpiece was built between 1845 and 1853, at a staggering cost of $342,000, and has long been at the center of the city's urban history. Constructed of bricks plastered and scored to look like stone, the building extends deeper than its narrow facade implies. Six fluted Ionic columns support the tympanum on the facade, which is decorated with bas-reliefs of Justice and Commerce by prolific Russian-American sculptor Robert A. Launitz.

A bronze statue of Benjamin Franklin outside Gallier Hall

Gallier Hall was built to serve as the headquarters of the Second Municipality when the city was briefly served by three separate governments. In 1852, it became City Hall, when the three were reunited. Many great historical figures have lain in state here, including Jefferson Davis, president of the Confederacy, and General Beauregard. Perhaps most notably, Gallier Hall was the venue for the city's official surrender to Union forces in the Civil War.

The building faces Lafayette Square, which was laid out in 1788 as Place Gravier, and renamed in 1824. The square contains statues of statesman Benjamin Franklin by Hiram Powers, and famed Senator Henry Clay by Joel T. Hart. John McDonogh, the great benefactor of the New Orleans public schools, is remembered with a statue by Atallio Piccirilli.

Today, the building is a popular vantage point during Mardi Gras (p66). VIP viewing galleries are erected for the carnival parades, which pause here to allow the marching bands to perform for the gathering crowds.

⑬ 🏈
Mercedes-Benz Superdome

📍 G7 ⌖ Sugar Bowl Drive 🚌 16 🚋 St Charles ⏱ For sporting events only 🌐 mbsuperdome.com

This vast landmark is home to local football teams the Saints and Tulane University's Green Wave. It is also the venue for the Sugar Bowl, the annual college football championships, and other sports and entertainment events. Built between 1971 and 1975, it occupies 52 acres, and stands 27 stories high.

The Superdome has become somewhat synonymous with the suffering of those affected by Hurricane Katrina. It was here that many thousands sought refuge from the flood waters. The building was severely damaged by wind, and flooding.

In September 2006, the Superdome reopened after a $193 million restoration. As the world's largest steel-constructed stadium that is unobstructed by posts, it has hosted the National Football

The flying saucer-shaped Mercedes-Benz Superdome glowing red at night

League Super Bowl seven times: the Super Bowl XLVII in 2013 being the most recent.

The **Smoothie King Center**, the "abydome," opened in 1999. In 2002, the Charlotte, North Carolina, Hornets professional basketball team moved here, becoming the home team, renamed the New Orleans Pelicans. The arena is also home to the Tulane University basketball team.

Smoothie King Center
 🏛 1501 Girod St
🖥 smoothiekingcenter.com

⑭
Saenger Theatre

🏛 H6 🏛 1111 Canal St
🚋 St Charles 🚌 3, 41
🖥 saengernola.com

Originally a cinema, this beautiful Italian Renaissance theater first opened in 1927. Once the flagship of brothers Julian and Abe Saenger's vast

empire, today it is one of only a handful of theaters that continue to operate under the Saenger name.

Designed by Emile Weil, it features an elegant mezzanine and towering arcade, while the main theater space is made to look like the courtyard of an Italian villa, with archways and statuary decorating the walls. The ceiling is accented by some 150 tiny lights, which resemble stars in the night sky.

Heavily damaged by the flood of 2005, the Saenger sat empty for years. New owners have returned this landmark building to its former glory, with additional state-of-the-art technology, and the theater reopened in 2013 to host touring Broadway shows, big-name comedians, and famous musicians.

Did You Know?
Julian and Abe Saenger once owned 320 theaters across the U.S. and the Caribbean.

STAY

Le Pavillon
One of the city's oldest hotels, renowned for the huge limestone pillars that grace its driveway. Impressive period artworks line the walls, hinting at its old-world elegance.

🏛 H7 🏛 833 Poydras St
🖥 lepavillon.com

$$ⓈⓈⓈ

The Old 77 Hotel and Chandlery
This converted chandelier factory now houses a trendy, art-focused hotel with the service levels to back up its looks, plus an enticing bar and restaurant.

🏛 H7 🏛 535 Tchoupitoulas St
🖥 old77hotel.com

$$ⓈⓈⓈ

The Eliza Jane
Another conversion (this time a print shop), this hotel has a wonderfully European ambience to it, a curated vintage feel to the rooms, and a fine French restaurant.

🏛 H7 🏛 315 Magazine St
🖥 hyatt.com
$$ⓈⓈⓈ

The Roosevelt Hotel
A grand old institution with an impressively decadent lobby. The standards here are high, and its Sazerac Bar is a piece of local history with stories aplenty.

🏛 H6 🏛 130 Roosevelt Way 🖥 theroosevelthotel.com

$$ⓈⓈⓈ

↑ A crowd going wild for Troy "Trombone Shorty" Andrews at the Saenger Theatre

Confederate Memorial Hall

H8 **929 Camp St at Howard Ave** **St Charles** **11, 41** **10am-5pm Tue-Sat** **Public hols** **confederatemuseum.com**

One of the oldest museums in the city, Confederate Memorial Hall offers a moving experience, telling the often tragic personal stories of the many young men who fought in the Civil War. Some were teenagers, like Landon Creek, who had fought in seven battles and was wounded three times by the age of 15. Several display cases contain objects relating to the occupation of the city by forces led by General

Benjamin "Beast" Butler, including a document, which came to be known as "The Woman Order," announcing that all women who insulted Union officers, sang Southern songs, or wore Confederate colors were to be locked up and treated as if they were "common harlots." The museum also holds a collection of items associated with Confederate president Jefferson Davis, from his cradle to his military boots. Several interesting exhibits are devoted to the black regiments that served during the war – some 180,000 African American soldiers enlisted to fight for the Union, roughly 10 per cent of the entire army.

The original Memorial Hall – a small, stately chamber featuring heavy trusses, gleaming cypress paneling, and detailed Romanesque architecture – was built in 1891 as a meeting place for Confederate veterans to reflect on their Civil War experiences and to house and protect their valuable relics, including bullets, guns, flags, paintings, uniforms, letters, and photographs.

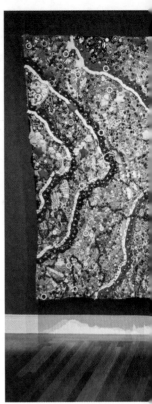

CONFEDERATE STATUES

As a Southern city, New Orleans has its fair share of statues erected to commemorate Confederate generals and the like. Many memorials were put up in the early twentieth century to reinforce Jim Crow laws, and some became rallying points in opposition to the African American civil rights movement in the 1950s and 1960s. In 2017, Mayor Mitch Landrieu began removing some of the more prominent statues, most famously that of General Robert E. Lee in Lee Circle. The decision was met with not a little resistance, with objectors using everything from law suits to firebombs to protect them. Landrieu saw it through, however, arguing that the monuments had promoted a "fictional, sanitized Confederacy."

New Orleans Contemporary Arts Center

H8 **900 Camp St** **St Charles** **11** **11am-5pm Wed-Mon** **Public hols** **cacno.org**

This warehouse-style center is the city's premier multidisciplinary space for contemporary arts, including dance, painting, video, performance art, theater, and music. Originally established in 1976, the Contemporary Arts Center (CAC) began its life as a community-led organization driven by a dedicated group of artists in New Orleans' burgeoning arts district.

The complex combines the original structure with modern designs to its full advantage, presenting a unique, modern space, mostly illuminated with natural light, that houses four galleries and two theaters. The rotating shows in the galleries usually remain for one or two months. The center offers year-round lectures, camps, and workshops for adults and children.

> **The Contemporary Arts Center began its life as a community-led organization driven by a dedicated group of artists in New Orleans' burgeoning arts district.**

The Little Gem Saloon

One of the city's few original jazz venues, this cool spot has been restored to its former glory, hosting live music by the bar every evening, and jazz brunches on Sundays.

⦿ H7
⌂ 445 Rampart St
ⓦ littlegemsaloon.com

The Sazerac Bar

Secret deals, prohibition drama, and women's liberation all play a part in the colorful history of this hotel bar. Sip a sazerac beneath the huge murals.

⦿ H6
⌂ Hotel Roosevelt, 130 Roosevelt Way
ⓦ winoschool.com

W.I.N.O

If you're a wine buff, you'll love this high-tech bar that lets you buy credit and then spend it via a chipped card on wines by the glass from its storage tanks.

⦿ J7
⌂ 610 Tchoupitoulas St
ⓦ winoschool.com

Shawne Major's 2008 work *Eating Cake* at the Ogden, and *(inset)* the museum's exterior

17 ✍ 〽️

Ogden Museum of Southern Art

⦿ H8 **⌂ 925 Camp St** **🚋 11 St Charles** **🕐 10am–5pm Wed–Mon, 10am–8pm Thu**
ⓦ ogdenmuseum.org

Opened in 2003, this museum is named for Roger H. Ogden, a philanthropist who donated the core collection of some 1,200 works by more than 400 Southern artists. The museum displays its artworks in a two-building complex connected by a corridor gallery. The Romanesque-style Howard Memorial Library was designed by Henry Hobson Richardson in 1888. This architectural masterpiece, with its splendid wood-panel rotunda, is incorporated into the more contemporary Goldring Hall. These two structures wrap around the Confederate Memorial Hall, so that the complex fronts Camp Street.

The museum has a variety of artwork from the 18th to the 21st century on show, and portrays the diversity of urban and rural life in the South from the Depression to the modern day. The collection includes works by William Henry Buck, Clarence Millet, John McCrady, George Dureau, Robert Gordy, and Ida Kohlmeyer.

On Thursdays, the Ogden After Hours series features live music, refreshments, book signings, and special exhibits.

A SHORT WALK
CENTRAL BUSINESS DISTRICT

Distance 1.2 miles (1.9 km) **Time** 25 minutes
Nearest Streetcar St. Charles Avenue

The hustle and bustle that surrounds daily activity in the downtown area extends throughout the Warehouse and Central Business District (CBD). As well as the historic 19th-century buildings that exist between a profusion of newer structures, there are residential streets, and old warehouses converted into stylish spaces housing jazz bars, restaurants, hotels, galleries, and museums. New Orleans' downtown is a hub of commerce, entertainment, dining, and shopping, and its lively wide streets make for pleasant, varied wandering.

At 750 Carondelet Street is the **Crescent Farmer's Market's** *CBD outpost. Each Saturday the lot buzzes with street food stands and stalls selling fresh local produce.*

Begin this walk by the St. Charles streetcar station on **Julia Street**. *This popular thoroughfare is known as "Gallery Row" for the many small art galleries lining it.*

Housed in a futuristic, brightly colored building, the **Ogden Museum of Southern Art's** *holds collections ranging from folk art to contemporary pieces (p135).*

The **Contemporary Arts Center** *was established in 1976 as one of the district's earliest spaces dedicated to the arts (p134). Today the complex promotes cutting-edge and experimental works*

GRAVIER STREET
PERDIDO STREET
O'KEEFE STREET
POYDRAS STREET
O'KEEFE STREET
BARONNE STREET
CARONDELET STREET
ST. CHARLES AVENUE
Crescent City Farmers Market
START
JULIA STREET
ST. JOSEPH ST
HOWARD AVENUE
Contemporary Arts Center
Ogden Museum of Southern Arts
CALLIOPE ST

← Admiring modern paintings at the Contemporary Arts Center

Locator Map
For more detail see p122

↑ Relaxing in Lafayette Square during
the Crescent Blues and BBQ Festival

*End this walk in grassy **Lafayette
Square**. Presided over by grand Gallier
Hall (p132), this is the city's second oldest
square. Today it plays host to the Crescent
Blues and BBQ Festival each autumn.*

*On Camp Street, peek inside
the impressive **St. Patrick's Church** to
admire its Gothic-inspired interior (p130).*

*At # 332, **LeMieux Galleries** is one of
dozens of art spaces lining Julia Street.
exhibiting fine contemporary works by
Louisiana artists.*

| 0 meters | | 300 | N |
| 0 yards | | 300 | ↑ |

*The **National
World War II
Museum** honors
the American con-
tribution to the war
effort, with huge
displays of planes,
ships, and military
memorabilia (p126).*

*Drop into **Cochon
Restaurant** on
Tchoupitoulas Street for
an elegant lunch. The
pork-heavy menu riffs
on traditional Cajun
flavors (p129).*

→ Enjoying Cajun-
inspired small plates
at Cochon Restaurant

GARDEN DISTRICT AND UPTOWN

In 1832, a residential quarter was established uptown on the former Livaudais Plantation. The land was subdivided and developed to create the city of Lafayette, which was incorporated into New Orleans in 1852. Here, between Jackson and Louisiana Avenues, and St. Charles Avenue and Magazine Street, wealthy merchants, planters, and bankers built mansions in a variety of styles, ranging from Greek Revival to Italianate to Queen Anne. The area became known as the Garden District because of the lush gardens that were laid out around the mansions. Settlement continued across Uptown as New Orleans annexed Jefferson City and Carrollton.

The city's uptown expansion was greatly enhanced by the opening of the St. Charles Avenue streetcar in 1835, which still runs from Canal Street to Carrollton Avenue. The 19th century also saw the establishment of the prestigious Tulane and Loyola universities, as well as the creation of Audubon Park out of the former Boré sugar plantation, bringing much-needed green space to the growing city.

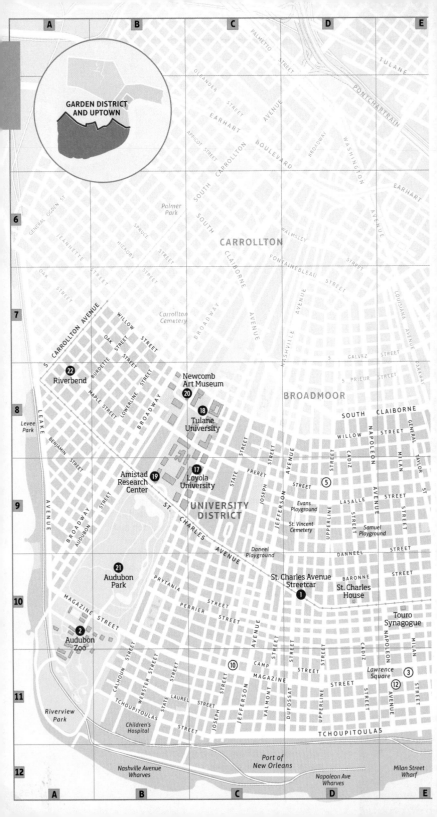

GARDEN DISTRICT AND UPTOWN

Must Sees
1. St. Charles Avenue Streetcar
2. Audubon Zoo

Experience More
3. Claiborne Cottage
4. Lafayette Cemetery
5. Briggs-Staub House
6. Robinson House
7. Southern Food and Beverage Museum
8. Toby's Corner
9. Carroll-Crawford House
10. Louise S. McGehee School
11. Mardi Gras World
12. Musson-Bell House
13. Colonel Short's Villa
14. Brevard-Wisdom-Rice House
15. Women's Guild Opera House
16. Payne-Strachan House
17. Loyola University
18. Tulane University
19. Amistad Research Center
20. Newcomb Art Museum
21. Audubon Park
22. Riverbend

Eat
1. Commander's Place
2. Stein's Deli
3. Shaya

Drink
4. Avenue Pub
5. Cure
6. Courtyard Brewery

Stay
7. The Pontchartrain Hotel
8. Henry Howard Hotel
9. The Columns Hotel

Shop
10. Hazelnut
11. Trashy Diva
12. Uptown Costume and Dancewear

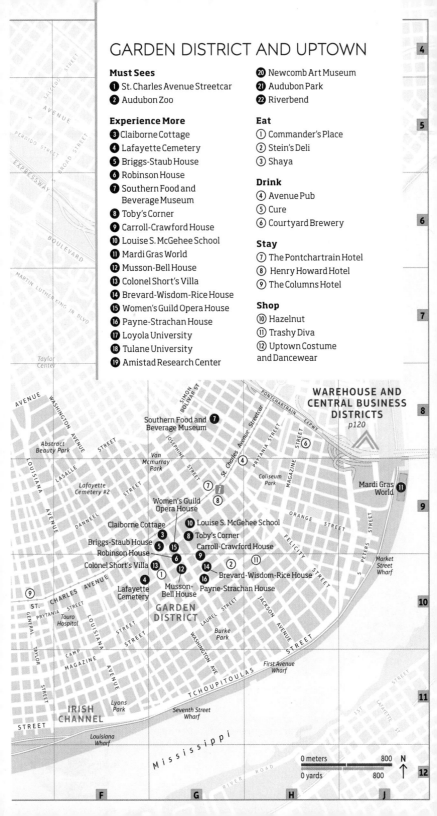

WAREHOUSE AND CENTRAL BUSINESS DISTRICTS
p120

ST. CHARLES AVENUE STREETCAR

📍 D10   🏠 St. Charles Avenue   🌐 norta.com

Board the beloved, olive-green St. Charles Avenue Streetcar for one of the city's most romantic rides. As you rumble uptown along Route 12, swaying in the handsome wooden seats, you'll pass city landmarks and decades of history.

Boarding the streetcar is like stepping back in time. A National Historic Landmark, this kind of car was immortalized by Tennessee Williams in his drama *A Streetcar Named Desire*. For a slow-moving romance, ride 6.5 miles (10 km) from Canal Street through the CBD, along tree-shaded St. Charles Avenue to Carrollton Avenue. You'll pass many famous landmarks, including Lafayette Square, the elegant 1850s St. Charles House, the Touro Synagogue, and Claiborne Cottage, a classic raised cottage built in 1857 for the daughter of the first American Louisiana governor. Due to electrical damage sustained during Hurricane Katrina, the St. Charles Avenue Streetcar was out of commission for two years. The return of its familiar green cars was greeted with delight by New Orleanians during the holiday season of 2007.

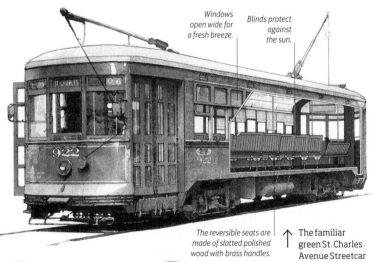

Windows open wide for a fresh breeze.

Blinds protect against the sun.

The reversible seats are made of slatted polished wood with brass handles.

↑ The familiar green St. Charles Avenue Streetcar

1867
Horse- and mule-power replaces the dirt and noise of the steam locomotives.

2005
Due to damage from Hurricane Katrina, service is suspended.

2014
▽ National Park Service lists the line as a National Historic Landmark.

1835
▲ The first steam-powered streetcars begin running; a dedicated right of way is later established.

1893
▲ Electric streetcars are installed and the line is extended along Carrollton Avenue.

1973
The St. Charles line is listed on the National Register of Historic Places.

Did You Know?

Opened in 1835, St. Charles Avenue is the world's oldest continuously operating streetcar line.

Boarding the trolley at Canal at Carondelet, on the way to Carrollton Avenue ↑

The entrance to Audubon Zoo, located in delightful City Park ↑

AUDUBON ZOO

📍 A10 🏠 6500 Magazine Street 🚋 St. Charles 🚌 11 🕐 10am–5pm Mon–Fri, 10am–6pm Sat & Sun ❌ First Fri in May, Thanksgiving, Dec 24–25, Mardi Gras 🌐 audubonnatureinstitute.org/zoo

Part of the highly respected Audubon Nature Institute, along with the Audubon Aquarium and the Audubon Insectarium, this world-class establishment traces its history back to the 19th century. Audubon Zoo is home to rare and endangered creatures, and its ethos centers around conservation and protecting natural habitats.

Landscaped with fountains and water gardens, this attractive 58-acre zoo is located in City Park (p176), and can be toured easily in a few hours. It opened in 1938 but was redesigned in the 1980s; today, the animals live in open paddocks that replicate their natural habitats. Only a few of the 1930s buildings remain. The award-winning Louisiana Swamp exhibit is one of the most engaging, showcasing Cajun culture and music alongside rare white alligators, who bask along the banks or float like logs in the muddy lagoon. Meanwhile in the African Savannah exhibit, rhinos, zebras, and white pelicans all live together with a host of opportunistic visitors such as ibis, heron, and egrets.

Did You Know?

Researching his major work, *The Birds of America*, John James Audubon identified 25 new species.

💬 INSIDER TIP
Make a Splash

After a stroll around the zoo, there's no better place to cool off than in the Cool Zoo. The Audubon's animal-themed water park, complete with its 750-ft (229-m) "Gator Run" lazy river, is popular with visitors of all ages.

→
Enjoying the water slides and soakers that keep the temperature down in the Cool Zoo

←
A tiger relaxing in the Asia enclosure, which also features elephants and leopards

→
A sun bear, the smallest of the bear species, climbing around the Asia exhibit

EXPERIENCE MORE

Claiborne Cottage

📍 G9 🏠 2524 St Charles Ave 🚋 St Charles 🚌 11, 14 🚫 To the public

The history of this Greek Revival-style cottage is somewhat disputed, but the plaque in front states that it was built in 1857 for Sophronie Claiborne Marigny, the daughter of the first governor of Louisiana. She was married to Mandeville Marigny, the youngest son of Bernard de Marigny, who introduced dice to the United States. The cottage variously served as a school, a convent, and a rectory throughout the first half of the 20th century. Later, it passed into the hands of the family of Anne Rice,

who would go on to become one of New Orleans' most successful authors with her gothic horror *Interview with the Vampire*. Rice would also use it as the setting of her 1997 novel *Violin*. In 2004 Rice sold Claiborne Cottage to entrepreneur and horse-breeder Evelyn B Benoit, who restored it to its former glory.

Lafayette Cemetery

📍 F10 🏠 1400 Washington Ave 🚋 St Charles 🚌 11, 14 🕐 7am–3pm daily 🚫 Public hols

This walled cemetery was laid out in 1833 by Benjamin Buisson to accommodate the residents of the adjacent Garden District. The second Protestant cemetery to open in New Orleans, it is the resting place of many German and British Protestants, as well as Americans who had migrated here from the east coast. By 1840 it was full, mostly with yellow fever victims, and a new cemetery was needed.

Among the notables buried here are Confederate General Harry T. Hays and Samuel Jarvis Peters (1801–85), an influential city politician and land developer. A Canadian, Peters arrived in New Orleans and quickly ascended to a powerful position by the time he was 30. He was one of the movers and shakers who developed the area above Canal Street, fashioning it into a Second Municipality comparable to the downtown Creole community below Canal Street. One of the most striking

> **In 2004 Rice sold Claiborne Cottage to entrepreneur and horse-breeder Evelyn B Benoit, who restored it to its former glory.**

💬 INSIDER TIP
Through the Keyhole

Although most of the mansions in the Garden District are private homes, you can tour some of them for one day a year. In December, the Holiday Home Tour, run by the Preservation Resource Center of New Orleans, sells tickets to fund their important work *(www.prcno.org)*.

← Tombs lining the walkways of Lafayette Cemetery amid lush greenery

memorials in this cemetery is the communal tomb built in 1852 to commemorate the Jefferson Fire Company #22. It is embellished with a typical pumper wagon.

The wall vaults or "ovens," a wall of inexpensive internment chambers, were added to the cemetery in 1858 to temporarily house the dead.

In Anne Rice's famous Gothic horror novel *Interview with the Vampire*, characters frequently wander around Lafayette Cemetery. This was also used prominently as a location in the film adaptation of the book. The author staged her own mock burial here in 1995 to promote her book, *Memnoch the Devil*.

---

⑤ Briggs-Staub House

📍 G9 🏠 2605 Prytania St
🚋 St Charles 🚌 11, 14
🚫 To the public

This mansion was built for gambler Cuthbert Bullitt by James Gallier Sr. in 1849. The house's Gothic Revival style is uncommon in this part of the city, because many Protestant Americans claimed it reminded them of Roman Catholic France. After Gallier had designed the building, Bullitt refused to pay for it, perhaps because of a gambling loss, and the house subsequently became the property of Charles Briggs, an English insurance executive.

---

⑥ Robinson House

📍 G10 🏠 1415 3rd St
🚋 St Charles 🚌 11, 14
🚫 To the public

One of the Garden District's grandest residences, this house was built for Virginia tobacco merchant Walter Robinson. Designed by Henry Howard, it was built between 1859 and 1865. The galleries of this Italian-style villa are supported with Doric columns on the first floor and Corinthian on the second. An unusual feature of this mansion is its curved portico, and it was one of the first buildings in the city to have indoor plumbing.

EAT

Commander's Palace
One of the city's most famous restaurants, serving up modern takes on local favorites. The lunch service features the ever-popular 25-cent Martinis.

📍 G10 🏠 1403 Washington Ave
🌐 commanders palace.com

💲💲💲

Stein's Deli
Get here early on the weekends for authentic New York-style deli sandwiches and bagels. There's a fine craft beer selection and excellent coffee pop-ups.

📍 G10 🏠 2207 Magazine St 🌐 steinsdeli.com

💲💲💲

Shaya
Come here for modern Israeli-inspired dishes and elegant small plates. Make sure to try the freshly baked pitta with silky smooth hummus and creamy baba ganoush.

📍 E11 🏠 4231 Magazine St
🌐 shayarestaurant.com

💲💲💲

↑ Imposing Briggs-Staub House, the Garden District's only Gothic Revival manison

STAY

Pontchartrain Hotel
Exudes 1950s glamor and has one of the best rooftop bars in the city.

◎G9
⌂2031 St. Charles Ave
ⓦthepontchartrain
hotel.com

⑤⑤⑤

Henry Howard Hotel
A debonair, mid-19th-century townhouse with a period feel.

◎G9 ⌂2041 Prytania St
ⓦhenryhoward
hotel.com

⑤⑤⑤

Columns Hotel
Fine Italianate architecture with an atmospheric veranda.

◎E10
⌂3811 St. Charles Ave
ⓦthecolumns.com

⑤⑤⑤

---

⑦

Southern Food and Beverage Museum

◎G8 ⌂1504 Oretha Castle Haley Blvd 🚋St. Charles
🕐11am–5.30pm Wed–Mon
ⓦnatfab.org/southern-food-and-beverage

A treasure trove for foodies, this delightful museum celebrates the food and drink of the American South and its starring role in the culture of the region. The former Dryades Market building provides an open, airy space for colorful displays that offer a fascinating insight into the iconic foods of New Orleans and beyond. The Gallery of the South features curated exhibits which highlight the food and foodways of 16 southern states. The Louisiana Gallery, for example, looks at sugar making, coffee drinking, crawfish harvesting and a range of dishes from beignets to jambalaya. On weekends, there are cooking demonstrations and other events.

The Museum of the American Cocktail is here too, showcasing popular drinks and their social history. Don't miss La Galerie de l'Absinthe for a look at the anise-flavored spirit. In the restaurant, you can have a cocktail from the city's oldest bar, renovated and installed here after being damaged in Hurricane Katrina.

---

⑧

Toby's Corner

◎G9 ⌂2340 Prytania St
🚋St. Charles 🚌11, 14, 27
🚫To the public

Built around 1838 and thought to be the Garden District's oldest residence, this house was built for Thomas Toby, a successful wheelwright who lost his fortune financing the cause for Texan independence from Mexico. It was, in fact, his wife who paid for the construction of the house. Toby subsequently worked as a plantation manager until he died.

After the Civil War, the house was auctioned off for $5,000. Now it is privately owned and closed to the public, but its facade is a superb example of the Greek Revival style.

↓ The Southern Food and Beverage Museum's expansive foyer

9
Carroll-Crawford House

⚲ G9 ⌂ 1315 First St
🚋 St. Charles 🚌 11, 14
🔒 To the public

This broadly proportioned house was built in 1869 for Joseph Carroll, a cotton merchant from Virginia. The surrounding gardens include venerable live oaks and other lush plantings. A two-story home with octagonal wings, the house is Italianate in design with fine cast-iron galleries.

The original carriage house can still be seen around the corner on Chestnut Street. The house's designer Samuel Jamison also constructed an identical building at 1331 First Street for rope dealer Joseph C. Morris.

10
Louise S. McGehee School

⚲ G9 ⌂ 2343 Prytania St
🚋 St. Charles 🚌 11, 14
🔒 To the public

James Freret designed this elaborate French Second Empire home in 1872 for sugar planter Bradish Johnson for $100,000. Freret had recently returned from Paris and was enamored of the École des Beaux-Arts, which is evident in this mansion's Renaissance Revival style. When it was built, the house incorporated all of the fashionable interior design elements and conveniences of the day: a conservatory, a marble pantry, a passenger elevator, and a magnificent circular staircase. It is one of the few houses in the city to have a basement.

Since 1929, it has served as a private school for girls. The cafeteria was once a stable, and the gym is a refurbished carriage house. Note the steep mansard roof with its wrought-iron parapet and the unique bull's-eye window on the

↑ Anthony, Cleopatra, and Elvis welcoming visitors to Blaine Kern's Mardi Gras World

facade. The gardens contain some magnificent magnolias and ginger trees.

11

Mardi Gras World

⚲ J9 ⌂ 1380 Port of New Orleans Place 🚋 Riverfront
🕐 9:30am–5:30pm daily
🌐 mardigrasworld.com

Blaine Kern is often called "Mr. Mardi Gras" because so many of the massive floats that roll through the streets during Carnival (p66) are constructed here in the 20 warehouse-dens of his company.

A tour of Mardi Gras World begins with a short film showing the floats in the parades and the stages of their production, from the original drawings to the manufacture of the final pieces. You can then don some costumes that krewe members have worn in past parades. Many of these are very heavy and ornate. Visitors can also wander one of the warehouses to view gigantic fiberglass and Styrofoam figures overlaid with papier-mâché. The cost of the floats is borne by the krewes themselves, with contributions from their members.

Did You Know?

Horse-drawn floats were introduced to Mardi Gras in 1840 by early carnival society, the Cowbellions.

Elegant ironwork of Italianate mansion, Musson-Bell House

Musson-Bell House

⊙ G10 🏠 1331 Third St
🚋 St. Charles 🚌 11, 14, 27
🚫 To the public

This handsome Italianate villa was built in 1853 for Michel Musson (1812–85), a successful and prominent Creole cotton merchant and the New Orleans postmaster. Musson had close ties with his extended family, including his sister Celestine Musson Degas, who lived in France. Celestine's son, Edgar Degas, was to become one of the world's great artists and a founder of the Impressionist movement.

After the Civil War, Edgar Degas came to visit Louisiana, but it is unlikely he ever saw this house. The war had dealt Musson's fortunes a severe blow and he sold the house in 1869, moving his family to rented accommodation on Esplanade Avenue (p174).

The house has eight bedrooms, seven bathrooms, a stable and carriage house, as well as a cistern for water storage on the roof. The facade is girdled by magnificent cast-iron galleries.

Colonel Short's Villa

⊙ G10 🏠 1448 Fourth St
🚋 St. Charles 🚌 11, 14, 27
🚫 To the public

Henry Howard designed this large Italian-style residence in 1859 for Kentuckian Colonel Robert Short. The veranda, with fine iron railings, extends around three sides of the house. An exquisite ironwork fence, incorporating a motif of morning glory and cornstalk, encloses the gardens (p152). The story goes that the Colonel had it installed to please his wife, who missed the cornfields of her native Iowa. Unlike a similar fence at Gauche Villa in the French Quarter (p96), famous for its detailed ironwork, this one has not been painted and shows its original colors. In September 1863, Union troops seized the residence, but it was returned to the family after the Civil War. Although closed to the public, the famous cornstalk fence is much visited.

Brevard-Wisdom-Rice House

⊙ G10 🏠 1239 First St
🚋 St. Charles 🚌 11, 14, 27
🚫 To the public

Fans of the Gothic author Anne Rice often stop to gawk at this stylish Greek Revival home, where she lived from 1989 to

2003. The house was designed for merchant Albert Hamilton Brevard in 1857 by James Calrow (who designed several other important houses in the Garden District) and cost some $13,000, at the time a formidable sum. Brevard-Wisdom-Rice House is adorned with ornate ironwork, including a fence incorporating a charming rose motif, earning the house its nickname, "Rosegate." Ionic and Corinthian columns support the galleries. The second owners of the property, the Clapp family, added the hexagonal wing in 1869. The gardens are splendid, featuring some stunning camellias.

Anne Rice, who was born in New Orleans and grew up in the Irish Channel, has portrayed the city in many of her best-selling *Vampire Chronicles* novels. She and her husband, poet-scholar Stan Rice, returned to New Orleans from San Francisco in 1988. Rice used this house as the setting for her occult horror novel *The*

> **Brevard-Wisdom-Rice House is adorned with ornate ironwork, including a fence incorporating a charming rose motif, earning the house its nickname, "Rosegate."**

Witching Hour (1990). She spent her teenage years living in Clairborne Cottage (*p146*) at 2524 St. Charles Avenue, which inspired much of her novel *Violin*. The author has restored several historic buildings, but after her husband died in 2003, Anne began to sell off her New Orleans properties.

15

Women's Guild Opera House

🅖 G9 🏠 2504 Prytania St
🚈 St. Charles 🚌 11, 14, 27
🕐 For tours by appt only
🌐 operaguildhome.org

William Freret designed the original Greek Revival section of this house, known as the Davis-Seebold Residence, in 1858 for a wealthy merchant. In 1965, it was bequeathed to the Women's Guild of the New Orleans Opera Association, a non-profit organizationg that preserves the rich opera traditions of New Orleans. It is now mainly used for meetings and receptions, but the house also features some exhibits relating to the history of opera in the city. In the 19th century, New Orleans was a major opera center, although its original French Opera house designed by James Gallier, Jr. burned down in 1919.

The octagonal tower of the Women's Guild Opera House, and a memorial plaque outside (*inset*) ↓

NEW ORLEANS IRONWORK

The shadows cast by New Orleans ironwork add a romantic touch to the city. Lacy galleries and artfully decorated gates are scattered across New Orleans' neighborhoods. The French Quarter is a particular focus for handmade Creole wrought iron, while the Garden District brims with sumptuous examples of cast iron.

WROUGHT IRON

Wrought iron came to the city before cast iron, in the early 19th century. Fashioned by hand into beautiful, fluid shapes by German, Irish, and Creole artisans, wrought ironing contains a purer metal, and is stronger than cast iron. The signature of New Orleans is its beautifully wrought Creole ironwork, which appears in many forms, including fences, gates, window grilles, balconies, hinges, doorknobs, and lanterns. It is particularly common in the French Quarter, where delicate ironwork balconies with unique designs and patterns were added to many buildings in the 1850s, influenced by the lacy galleries of Spanish architecture.

Wrought-iron balconies depicting oak leaves and acorns can be seen on the LaBranche House on Royal Street (p70).

> **Fashioned by hand into beautiful, fluid shapes by German, Irish, and Creole artisans, wrought ironing contains a purer metal, and is stronger than cast iron.**

CORNSTALK FENCES

New Orleans has three "cornstalk" fences, so-called because of their decorative cast-iron motifs featuring ears of corn, along with swirls of morning glory, swans, and pumpkins. Each of these fences are designs by the Wood & Perot foundry. One is at 915 Royal Street's Cornstalk Hotel (p98), another at Colonel Short's Villa in the Garden District (p150), and a third is at the Dufour-Plassan house on the corner of White and Bell streets in Faubourg St. John.

CAST IRON

Cast iron was poured into wooden molds and allowed to set - as a result it has a solid, fixed appearance. However the material's greater plasticity meant that it could be shaped into ornate, raised relief designs, like the many found adorning homes in the Garden District. Favored as superior to wood as they withstood humidity, cast-iron designs could also be reproduced on a mass scale. The Pontalba Buildings, commissioned by Baroness Pontalba, spurred on the craze for ironwork (p77) in the 1850s, with some of the patterns designed by the Baroness's son.

IRONWORK MOTIFS

In the 1850s, Philadelphia iron-mongers Wood & Perot opened a branch office in New Orleans. Offering hundreds of patterns specially designed for the city, the company quickly grew, its motifs including abstracts, acorns, fruits, cherubs, vines, and animals. These were soon seen in railings throughout the city.

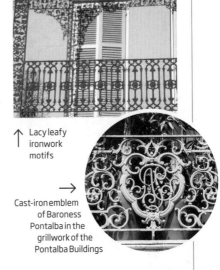

↑ Lacy leafy ironwork motifs

→ Cast-iron emblem of Baroness Pontalba in the grillwork of the Pontalba Buildings

16

Payne-Strachan House

G10 🏠 **1134 First St**
🚋 **St. Charles** 🚌 **11, 14, 27**
🚫 **To the public**

This grand Neo-Classical home was built in the 1850s by Judge Jacob U. Payne, who brought over slaves from his plantation in Kentucky and had them construct it by hand. The two-story Greek Revival residence features Ionic columns on the first gallery and Corinthian on the second. The house passed to Payne's son-in-law, Charles Erasmus Fenner, a close friend of Jefferson Davis, United States senator and president of the Confederacy. Davis died here on December 6, 1889, in the first-floor guest room.

A striking aspect of the house is the sky-blue ceiling in the gallery, the color having been chosen in the belief that it

↑ Neo-Classical Payne-Strachan House, where Jefferson Davis spent his last days

would keep winged insects from nesting there and would also ward off evil spirits. In fact, many homes in the neighborhood follow this superstition.

17

Loyola University

C9 🏠 **6363 St Charles Ave** 🚋 **St. Charles** 🚌 **15, 22** 🕐 **9am–7pm daily** 🌐 **loyno.edu**

The Jesuit Order established the College of the Immaculate Conception downtown in 1840. It merged with Loyola College, becoming Loyola University in 1912. The Tudor-Gothic buildings house the largest Catholic university in the South. The three buildings facing St. Charles Avenue are Marquette Hall, the oldest building on campus; the adjacent Thomas Hall, a former residence and chapel for the Jesuits; and the Most Holy Name of Jesus Roman Catholic Church, whose design was inspired by Canterbury Cathedral in the UK.

Notable Loyola alumni include former NASA administrator Sean O'Keefe, longtime *Simpsons* voice actor and Spinal Tap bassist Harry Shearer, and singer Harry Connick, Jr. The statue of Jesus with uplifted arms in front of Marquette Hall is referred to locally as "Touchdown Jesus," for obvious reasons.

← The elaborate Tudor-Gothic facade of Loyola University

18,000

undergraduate and postgraduate students attend the Tulane and Loyola universities.

Library houses the Hogan Jazz Archive, plus other special collections.

---

⑲
Amistad Research Center

⊙ B9 ⌂ Tilton Hall, Tulane University 🚋 St. Charles ⊞ 15, 22 🕐 8:30am–4:30pm Mon-Fri, 9am-1pm Sat ⓦ amistadresearch center.org

This research center is named for the famous slave mutiny aboard the Cuban slave ship *Amistad* in 1839. After a trial in Hartford, Connecticut, the slaves were acquitted and allowed to return home.

The American Missionary Association, an organization formed to defend the slaves, established the center's archive, which moved to New Orleans in 1969. It consists of documents, photos, pamphlets, and oral history records. A small gallery showcases artists including such names as Henry O. Tanner and Elizabeth Catlett.

---

⑱
Tulane University

⊙ C8 ⌂ 6823 St Charles Ave 🚋 St. Charles ⊞ 15, 22 🕐 9am-5pm daily ⓦ tulane.edu

Founded in 1834 as a medical college, the precursor of Tulane University was given its new name in 1882 after receiving a substantial gift from Paul Tulane, a native of Princeton, New Jersey. He made a fortune from running a merchandising business, which he launched in New Orleans in 1822. Tulane's School of Business is the oldest college of commerce in the United States.

The university moved to its current location in 1894. The 110-acre campus has 79 buildings, designed in a variety of styles. The Howard Tilton Memorial

SHOP

Hazelnut
This store has a great selection of home goods and gifts, and is owned by Bryan Batt, who famously played Salvatore Romano in the TV show *Mad Men*.

⊙ C11 ⌂ 5525 Magazine St ⓦ hazelnut neworleans.com

Trashy Diva
A homegrown success story, this women's fashion store specializes in retro patterns, and elegant dresses and lingerie.

⊙ H10 ⌂ 2048 Magazine St ⓦ trashydiva.com

Uptown Costume and Dancewear
Where locals come for last-minute costume inspiration. Perfect for Mardi Gras or Halloween.

⊙ E11 ⌂ 4326 Magazine St 📞 895-7969

⑳

Newcomb Art Museum

📍 B8 🏛 Tulane University
📞 865-5328 🚋 St. Charles
🚌 15, 22 🕐 10am-5pm
Tue-Fri, 11am-4pm Sat
& Sun 🚫 Public hols and
summer months

In 1886, Josephine Le Monnier Newcomb founded a women's college that was allied with Tulane University. Initially, she donated $100,000 in memory of her daughter Harriot Sophie Newcomb, who died at age 15 in 1870. When Josephine herself died, she left an estate of over $2.5 million to the college. The Woldenberg Art Center houses the Newcomb Art Museum and a smaller space to display student and faculty works. The Newcomb Museum focuses on traveling shows and curates its own exhibitions.

The name of Newcomb is more familiarly associated with the arts-and-crafts style of pottery that was made at the Newcomb College of Art from 1895 to 1940. The gallery has some typical pieces on display.

㉑

Audubon Park

📍 B10 🏠 6500 Magazine St
🚋 St. Charles 🚌 11, 22
🌐 auduboninstitute.org

This park was carved out of the plantations owned by the Foucher and Boré families in 1871. In 1884, the World's Industrial and Cotton Exposition was held here, helping to boost the city's morale at a time when New Orleans was still recovering from the double devastations of the Civil War and Reconstruction (p52). The exposition's main building alone covered almost four times the surface of the Superdome (p132), and it was here that the first streetcar was introduced to the city. During the festivities, the Mardi Gras Krewe of Rex (p66) arrived aboard a yacht, establishing a tradition that survives to this day.

In the park there are several ponds which host myriad bird species, along with recreation areas, sports facilities, and Audubon Zoo (p144). With the Zoo, Aquarium (p124), and

---

> 📷 PICTURE PERFECT
> ### Say "Trees"
>
> Deep within Audubon Park is the ancient Étienne de Boré Oak, or "Tree of Life," a southern live oak tree thought to be around 500 years old. The tree's gnarled trunk, rippling roots, and vast canopy make it a popular spot for wedding ceremonies and set the backdrop for the perfect snap.

↑ Audubon Park fountain, and *(inset)* an egret nesting on one of the park's many ponds

DRINK

Avenue Pub

The city doesn't have too many dedicated pubs, but Avenue always has around 40 excellent beers on tap, rotated often enough to keep you coming back. The kitchen won't disappoint either.

📍 G8
🏠 1732 St. Charles Ave
🌐 theavenuepub.com

Cure

New Orleans is the spiritual home of the cocktail, and they don't get better than at this chic craft-cocktail bar. Peruse the innovative menu or let the skilled mixologists guide you.

📍 D9 🏠 4905 Freret St
🌐 curenola.com

Courtyard Brewery

Micro-breweries are sprouting up across the city, and this Garden District venture is one of the best, serving up its own tasty brews. A range of rotating street food trucks complement the drinks.

📍 H8 🏠 1620 Erato St
🌐 courtyard
brewing.com

the Butterfly House and Insectarium *(p131)* the park forms part of the Audubon Nature Institute, named for naturalist John James Audubon, whose statue stands in its grounds. Audubon, the artist of *Birds of America*, was born in the West Indies. He came to New Orleans and rented his first studio in 1821 at 706 Barracks Street. He stayed only four months before taking off for a brief sojourn as tutor at Oakley Plantation in West Feliciana Parish. Here, in this rich ornithological environment, he began many of his renowned bird portraits, but due to a dispute with his employer, quickly returned to New Orleans and took up residence at another studio at 505 Dauphine Street.

22 Riverbend

📍 A8 🏠 Riverfront of St. Charles Ave
🚋 St. Charles 🚌 34

With more than 300 billion gallons of water flowing by the city each day, New Orleans lives under the constant threat of flood. A system of spillways, pumps, and levees, like this one along the riverfront of St. Charles Avenue, forms a line of defense against the temperamental Mississippi. Still, certain sections of the city are prone to flooding, particularly after heavy rains. The pumping system was installed soon after 1927 when the city was so threatened that the authorities cut the levee

below the city in St. Bernard Parish to forestall urban flooding. This part of the levee has been adapted as a recreation area, where visitors can enjoy a beautiful view of the river. The laid-back Riverbend neighborhood, dotted with locally owned restaurants, cafés, and shops, is perfect for an unhurried stroll. Browse through vintage boutiques on Maple Street or peruse second-hand books on Oak Street.

A SHORT WALK
GARDEN DISTRICT

Distance 0.4 miles (0.6 km) **Time** 10 minutes
Nearest Streetcar St. Charles Avenue

When Americans arrived in New Orleans, they settled upriver from the French Quarter. The plantations that lined St. Charles Avenue in the 1820s were subdivided and the city of Lafayette established. It was incorporated into New Orleans in 1852. Today, this area is referred to as the Garden District, a residential neighborhood, home to the great, Gothic Lafayette Cemetery, and filled with grand Victorian mansions built by wealthy city merchants and planters. The gardens, planted with magnolia, camellia, sweet olive, jasmine, and azalea, are as stunning as the residences themselves.

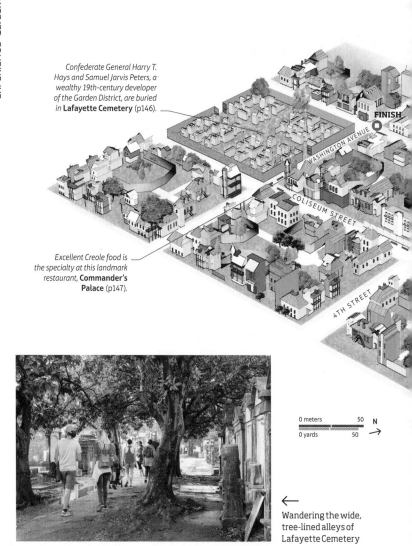

Confederate General Harry T. Hays and Samuel Jarvis Peters, a wealthy 19th-century developer of the Garden District, are buried in **Lafayette Cemetery (p146).**

FINISH

WASHINGTON AVENUE

COLISEUM STREET

4TH STREET

Excellent Creole food is the specialty at this landmark restaurant, **Commander's Palace (p147).**

0 meters 50   N
0 yards 50   →

← Wandering the wide, tree-lined alleys of Lafayette Cemetery

Colonel Short's Villa, with its decorative filigree veranda and cornstalk fence

Locator Map
For more detail see p140

Built in 1859 for Colonel Robert Short of Kentucky and designed by Henry Howard, **Colonel Short's Villa** (p150) *is known for its exquisite cornstalk fence (p153).*

The handsome Gothic Revival **Briggs-Staub House** *(p147) was designed by James Gallier, Sr. in 1849.*

Claiborne Cottage *was built in 1857 for the daughter of the first American governor of Louisiana (p146).*

ST. CHARLES AVENUE

PRYTANIA STREET

START ▶

3RD STREET

Musson-Bell House *was the home of Michel Musson, uncle of artist Edgar Degas (p150). Its lacy galleries were added by a later owner, an iron merchant.*

One of the Garden District's grandest residences, **Robinson House** *was built between 1859 and 1865 for Virginia tobacco merchant Walter Robinson (p147).*

A LONG WALK

LOWER GARDEN DISTRICT

Distance 1.75 miles (2.8 km) **Time** 30 minutes
Nearest Streetcar St. Charles Avenue

With its mix of mansions, markets, boutiques, and cafés, the Lower Garden District offers visitors a sample of the influences at play in the city through the last two centuries. Although this area is not as opulent as the neighboring Garden District, it has seen tremendous revitalization since the 1990s. This walk takes you along wide, shaded avenues past historic buildings, ornate churches, an antebellum mansion, and a cut-down version of the Eiffel Tower.

Locator Map
For more detail see p140

GARDEN
DISTRICT AND
UPTOWN Lower
Garden District

0 meters   300   N
0 yards   300   ↑

At the end of this walk, on the corner of **St. Andrew Street***, is a streetcar stop for the return trip downtown on the St. Charles Avenue streetcar line.*

At No. 2040, you'll find the striking **Eiffel Society** *building, formed from pieces of the Paris landmark removed during its 1980 renovation and shipped here.*

At No. 2220 St. Charles Avenue is the **House of Broel***, an antebellum and High Victorian mansion open to the public for tours.*

St. Charles Avenue *is the main route for Mardi Gras parades (p66): look up and you might spot carnival beads tangled in the branches of the oaks along the street.*

At No. 1239 7, is **Brevard-Wisdom-Rice House** *(p150), a private home previously owned by novelist Anne Rice and the setting for her book The Witching Hour.*

At No. 1134 1st Street, is the privately owned **Payne-Strachan House** *(p154), where Jefferson Davis, president of the American Confederacy, died in 1889.*

FINISH

Eiffel Society

House of Broel

Louise S. McGehee School

Toby's Corner

Women's Opera Guild House

Carroll Crawford House

Brevard-Wisdom Rice House

Robinson House

Payne Strachan House

↑ The 1850s Greek Revival-style Brevard-Wisdom-Rice House

Strolling down Magazine Street, with its boutiques and vintage stores →

Begin at the streetcar stop at **St. Charles Avenue** and Melpomene Street, which is one of a collection of parallel streets in the area, named for the Nine Muses of Greek mythology.

START ▶

Head toward the river to **Coliseum Park**. Laid out in 1806, the park's name refers to an outdoor arena that was planned here but never realized. Continue along Camp Street beneath shady oak trees.

Dominating this corner of Magazine Street is **St. Vincent's Guesthouse**, with its fanciful wrought-iron balconies. The inn was originally built as an orphanage in 1861 during epidemics of yellow fever.

Continue up **Magazine Street**, where homes give way to rows of boutiques and restaurants with large balconies shading the sidewalks beneath.

Constance Street is home to two historic Catholic churches built in the mid-19th century. The first, the Irish **St. Alphonsus** is now an arts and cultural center with tours available.

The second of Constance Street's churches is **St. Mary's Assumption**. Much of the ornate interior decoration of this German Baroque Revival church was imported from Munich.

↑ St. Mary's Assumption, a German Catholic church

MID-CITY

Extending from the French Quarter toward Lake Pontchartrain, Mid-City is the greenest part of New Orleans. Because it stands on low-lying terrain once known as the "backswamp," this was one of the last neighborhoods to be developed in the latter 19th and early 20th centuries. A great swath of this district is occupied by City Park. Carved out of the former Allard Plantation, the land was purchased in 1845 by bank director John McDonogh from the bankrupt Allard family. Upon McDonogh's death in 1850, the land was donated to the city, on the provision that the funds from its sale be used for public schools. Instead, the city bent the rules a little and created a park. NOMA, the city's oldest fine arts institution, was established here in 1911 by Isaac Delgado, a wealthy sugar broker. The other green areas in Mid-City are given over to cemeteries such as Greenwood, Metairie, St. Louis Cemetery #3, and Cypress Grove. Laid out in the mid-19th century, ornate, above-ground tombs and mausoleums became the final resting places of prominent New Orleanians.

Architecturally and culturally diverse, today Mid-City runs the gamut from characterful bars and eateries to colorful shotgun houses and stately homes.

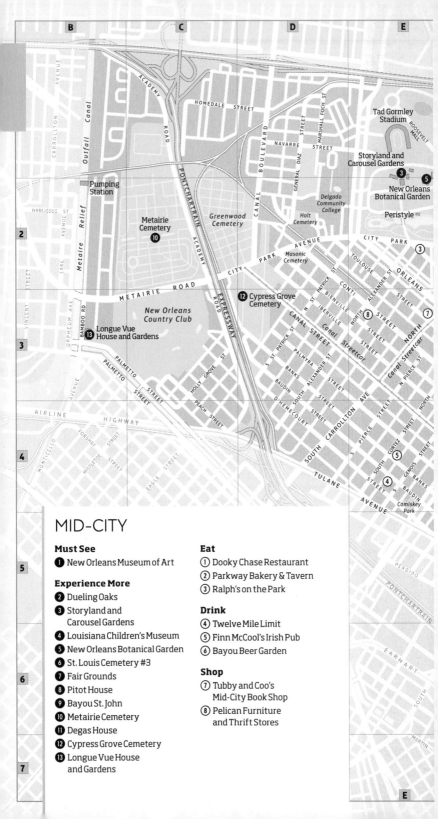

MID-CITY

Must See

❶ New Orleans Museum of Art

Experience More

❷ Dueling Oaks
❸ Storyland and Carousel Gardens
❹ Louisiana Children's Museum
❺ New Orleans Botanical Garden
❻ St. Louis Cemetery #3
❼ Fair Grounds
❽ Pitot House
❾ Bayou St. John
❿ Metairie Cemetery
⓫ Degas House
⓬ Cypress Grove Cemetery
⓭ Longue Vue House and Gardens

Eat

① Dooky Chase Restaurant
② Parkway Bakery & Tavern
③ Ralph's on the Park

Drink

④ Twelve Mile Limit
⑤ Finn McCool's Irish Pub
⑥ Bayou Beer Garden

Shop

⑦ Tubby and Coo's Mid-City Book Shop
⑧ Pelican Furniture and Thrift Stores

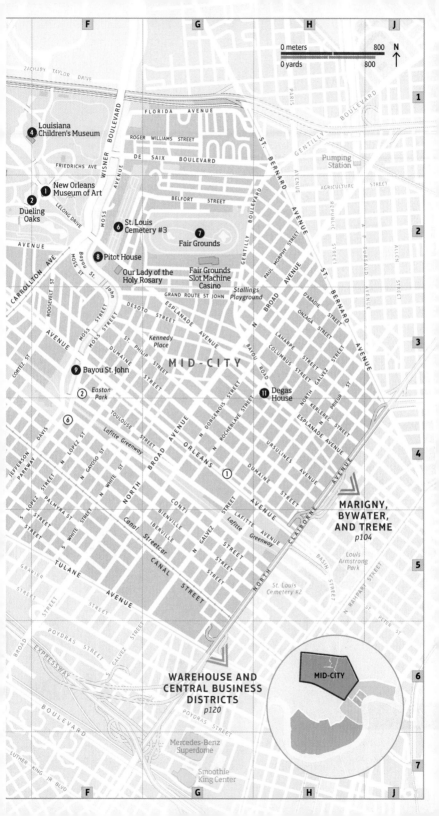

NEW ORLEANS MUSEUM OF ART

📍F2 🏛1 Collins Diboll Circle, City Park 🚌46, 48 🕐Museum: 10am-6pm Tue-Thu, 10am-9pm Fri, 10am-5pm Sat, 11am-5pm Sun; Besthoff Sculpture Garden: 9am-6pm daily 🚫Public hols 🌐noma.org

Together, the New Orleans Museum of Art (NOMA) and the adjacent Sydney and Walda Besthoff Sculpture Garden comprise one of the most important cultural destinations in the Gulf South. Housed in a grand Neo-Classical building in New Orleans City Park, NOMA'S collection includes art from the Renaissance to the modern era.

For over a century, NOMA has been the city's principle fine arts institution. Its impressive permanent collections and rotating exhibits rival those found in the best museums in the country. Visitors to NOMA can view works by Picasso, Degas, Miró, Rodin, and Pollock; a 10,000-piece photography collection; and Asian, African, and American art. In a beautiful 11-acre (4.45-hectare) site, the sculpture garden showcases pieces by world-renowned artists, such as Henry Moore and Barbara Hepworth.

Did You Know?

Surrounding the museum, the Besthoff Sculpture Garden holds more than 90 sculptures.

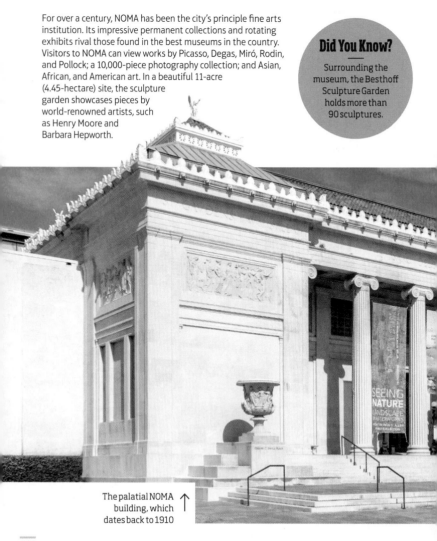

The palatial NOMA building, which dates back to 1910

Joel Shapiro's bronze *Untitled* (1991) on display in the Besthoff Sculpture Garden

→
The resplendent lobby at NOMA, which leads to numerous rooms of sublime art

THE BESTHOFF SCULPTURE GARDEN

The dynamic sculptures of Henry Moore, Barbara Hepworth, Louise Bourgeois, George Segal, and other renowned artists are displayed among the ancient oaks, magnolias, and tranquil lagoons of the Sydney and Walda Besthoff Sculpture Garden. The original garden, adjacent to the museum building, opened in 2003, with an expansion in 2019 seeing the site double in size to include an amphitheater, pedestrian bridges, and 26 new works. Visitors can wander around the park, or join one of the daily tours.

↑ Admiring Renaissance paintings in the NOMA's European Collection

↑ *Portrait of a Young Woman* (1918) by Amideo Modigliani, displayed in one of the first-floor European galleries

Exploring the New Orleans Museum of Art

The museum has expanded from exhibiting just nine pieces of art when it opened in 1911 to displaying almost 40,000 works over three floors today. Major collections in NOMA's 46 galleries include a vast selection of works of European art, which is spread across the first and second floors, from 12th-century Italian Florentine to 20th-century French and Spanish works. There are specialized collections of Latin American and Prehispanic art; American Indian works; arts of Africa and Asia; photography; and decorative arts, on the second and third floors. Modern art enthusiasts are catered for in a display located on the second floor, which covers all the major 20th-century American and European movements.

> The museum has expanded from exhibiting just nine pieces of art when it opened in 1911 to displaying almost 40,000 works over three floors today.

Museum Collections

African and Oceanic Art

▷ This is one of the finest African art collections in the country. It features figures, sculptures, ancient terracottas, textiles, furniture, masks, costumes, marionettes, and musical instruments. One highlight is a rare palace veranda post carved in the shape of an equestrian warrior figure. The Oceania gallery includes wooden figures from Papua New Guinea and Maori ornaments.

Art of the Americas

North, Central, and South American art are the focus here, with works spanning Latin America, and the United States. Works range from Mayan artifacts and pre-Columbian artworks, right through to the Spanish-Colonial period. The section also includes some fine examples of early American artists, a collection of Louisiana paintings, and American Indian art from ancient times to the present day.

Contemporary Art

◁ A great variety of sculpture, paintings, and mixed-media works are included in the Contemporary Art collection, which encompasses contemporary European art and the American art exhibits.

Asian Art

NOMA began its collection of Asian art in 1914 with a selection of Chinese jade and stone carvings. The Asian Art galleries contain one of the finest collections of Edo (1600-1868) Japanese paintings. All the major Japanese schools are represented, particularly the Nanga, Zenga, and Maruyama-Shijo schools. The collection also includes a wide variety of ceramics, lacquer, textiles, prints, and photographs.

Decorative Arts

▷ More than 15,000 works comprise this distinctive collection, which includes more than 6,000 glass items, furniture, and miniature portraits. The pottery collection features pieces from New Orleans' own Newcomb Pottery and a rare collection of "Old Paris" porcelain.

European Art

The European collection spans a period of 600 years and features examples from the major national schools. The Kress Collection includes sublime Italian Old Master paintings from the early Renaissance to the 18th century. Dutch, Flemish, and Impressionist works are also showcased, with French art well represented in the form of several works from the 17th to the 20th centuries. Among them are a number of paintings by Impressionist Edgar Degas, who visited New Orleans in the 1870s.

Photography, Prints, and Drawings

These rotating collections consist of more than 20,000 objects including prints, books, and unique works on paper that are displayed in a special suite of galleries. This department has two exhibitions a year. Highlights of the collection include works by French artist Henri Matisse.

TOP 4 COLLECTION HIGHLIGHTS

Mounted Warrior Veranda Post (c. 1910-14)
A rare carving by Yoruba artist Olowe of Ise.

Standing Ganesha (12th-13th century)
A beautiful Indian stone carving of the Hindu elephant-headed god.

Reclining Mother and Child (1975)
Henry Moore's elegant work of maternal love.

Portrait of Marie Antoinette (c. 1788)
One of Vigée Le Brun's sympathetic portraits of Marie Antoinette.

EXPERIENCE MORE

❷ Dueling Oaks

⬚E1 ⒶCity Park ⬚Canal
⬚46, 48, 90

Behind an imposing statue of Confederate General P. G. T. Beauregard, which guards the entrance to City Park, Lelong Avenue approaches the New Orleans Museum of Art. To the left is a grand, solitary oak, still called the Dueling Oaks, although there is now only one.

Many duels were fought in New Orleans, and most of these took place in the bosky acres of what has since become City Park. Under the massive branches of the live oaks, as many as ten duels a day were fought. Reports indicate that one particular dueler insisted on using whaling harpoons to settle the dispute, after which the offended party decided he wasn't so offended after all. The last duel was fought in 1939 between two students from a local fencing academy. The owner of the original plantation from which City Park was carved, Louis Allard, is rumored to be buried at the foot of the oaks.

❸ Storyland and Carousel Gardens

⬚E2 ⒶCity Park ⬚Canal
⬚46, 48, 90 ⬚10am- 4pm Tue–Fri, 11am-6pm Sat & Sun ⬚Dec 25 ⬚neworleanscitypark.com

Storyland, a beguiling theme park for children, is filled with all kinds of entertainments derived from traditional folk tales and well-known nursery rhymes. Kids can enjoy Jack and Jill's slide, climb around Miss Muffet's spider web, or challenge Captain Hook to a duel. Along the way, they may also encounter fairytale characters such as Jack (of the Beanstalk), Puss in Boots, Rapunzel, and many others. There is also story reading, puppet shows in the Puppet Castle, and face painting.

The carousel, situated in the southwest corner of the gardens, was built in 1906 and is one of the few antique wooden carousels left in the U.S. Nearby, visitors can climb aboard a miniature train, which has run around the park since 1896. A large Ferris wheel offers a bird's-eye view of the park.

❹   Louisiana Children's Museum

⬚E1 Ⓐ1 Roosevelt Mall
⬚St Charles ⬚10, 11
⬚9:30am-4:30pm Tue-Sat, noon-4:30pm Sun
⬚Public hols ⬚lcm.org

This activity-oriented museum allows children to entertain themselves with a variety of role-playing games, plus other interactive exhibits

TOP 4 CITY PARK SPORTS

Tennis
City Park Pepsi Tennis Center has 26 lighted courts, which can be reserved in advance.

Golf
The Practice Center has a 74-tee lighted driving range and an 18-hole putting course with water features.

Boating
The park's 8 miles (13 km) of lagoons provide ample opportunities for boating, and bass and trout fishing.

Horse Riding
City Park's Equest Stables offer riding lessons and trail rides.

↑ Riding the antique wooden horses at the Storyland and Carousel Gardens

↑ The Botanical Garden's lily pond and Pavilion of the Two Sisters, and *(inset)* seasonal displays

with a didactic focus. The museum relocated to City Park in mid-2019, its new lagoon-side site encompassing play areas and nature exhibits, and galleries where kids can explore the journey of food from field to fork, along with a literacy center, two cafés, and sensory and edible gardens.

5 ⊘ 🏛

New Orleans Botanical Garden

📍 E1 🚪 Victory Ave, City Park 🚋 Canal 🚌 46, 48, 90 🕐 10am–4:30pm Tue-Sun 🚫 Jan 1, Dec 25, Mardi Gras 🌐 neworleanscitypark.com

This 10-acre public garden was created in the 1930s. Back then, it was mainly a rose garden, but today there are more than 2,000 varieties of plants from around

the world, with aquatics, native and tropical plants, ornamental trees, shrubs, perennials, and much more inside various theme gardens.

The Garden Study Center and the Pavilion of the Two Sisters are reminiscent of European garden architecture. The Conservatory houses orchids and two major exhibits: Living Fossils, showcasing fossilized plants that grew on the earth before flowering plants, and the impressive Tropical Rainforest exhibit, with educational displays of geckos, tree frogs, and snakes.

The splendid Enrique Alférez Sculpture Garden features several works by the beloved Mexican-American artist surrounded by ornate shrubs, vibrant cherry blossoms, and an ancient live oak tree, including his *Women in Huipil* and *The Flute Player*.

Much of the plant collection was lost under several feet of water as a result of Hurricane Katrina, but the gardens were completely rebuilt in little more than six months with the help of volunteers and donors.

EAT

Dooky Chase Restaurant
Sample Creole comfort food classics of gumbo and fried chicken at this legendary New Orleans institution.

📍 G4 🏠 2301 Orleans Ave 🌐 dookychase restaurant.com

$$$

Parkway Bakery and Tavern
One of the many must-eat places in town, renowned for their take on the po'boy sandwich.

📍 F3 🏠 538 Hagan Ave 🌐 parkwaypoorblys.com

$$$

Ralph's on the Park
Fine dining with wonderful views of City Park in a building that dates back to the 1860s.

📍 E2 🏠 900 City Park Ave 🌐 ralphsonthepark.com

$$$

→
Wandering St. Louis Cemetery #3, one of the city's largest graveyards

6

St. Louis Cemetery #3

Q F2 **🏠** 3421 Esplanade Ave **☎** 482-5065 **🚌** 48, 90 **🕐** 8am–4:30pm Mon–Sat, 8am–4pm Sun **🎭** Mardi Gras

This pristine cemetery, with its beautiful wrought-iron gates, opened in 1856. Among the notable figures buried here is Antoine Michoud, the original owner of a plantation which is now the site of the NASA Michoud Assembly Facility where the Saturn rocket booster was constructed in the 1960s. There is also a memorial to architect

James Gallier, Sr. *(p132)* and his wife, who are buried in Metairie Cemetery *(p174)*. Both were tragically killed when the steamer *Evening Star* sank en route from New York to New Orleans in October 1866.

Other famous figures here include Father Rouquette, missionary to the Choctaw, and black Creole philanthropist Thomy Lafon, the owner of the old Orleans Ballroom who also sponsored an orphanage for African American children.

Less visited than #1 and #2, St. Louis Cemetery #3 is perfect for taking a quiet stroll and gathering your thoughts.

JAZZFEST

What started in 1970 as a local celebration in Louis Armstrong Park, the New Orleans Jazz and Heritage Festival, or Jazz Fest, is now a major player on the festival circuit. Held at the Fair Grounds since 1972, today hundreds of thousands attend to hear international jazz and pop music acts, from Herbie Hancock to Elton John *(www.nojazzfest.com)*.

7

Fair Grounds

Q G2 **🏠** 1751 Gentilly Blvd **🚌** 48 **w** fairgrounds racecourse.com

In the mid-1800s, New Orleans was a leading center for horse racing. The "Louisiana Race Course" – later the "Union Race Course" and "Creole Race Course" – operated in the 19th century on what would later become the Fair Grounds, making it one of the oldest racetracks in North America. When the Metairie Racecourse (now Metairie Cemetery) closed, the Louisiana Jockey Club took over and purchased the Luling Mansion just off Esplanade as a clubhouse. The name change occurred when the Fair Grounds Corporation took over in 1940.

Races are generally run here from November to March, culminating in the prestigious Louisiana Derby, a major preparatory race for the Kentucky Derby. The Fair Grounds also hosts the annual New Orleans Jazz Festival, usually at the end of April or the beginning of May. The track also has a slot machine casino that is open year round.

8

Pitot House

📍 F2 🏠 1440 Moss St
🚋 Canal 🚌 46, 48, 90
🕐 10am–3pm Wed–Sat
🚫 Public hols
🌐 pitothouse.org

This classic West Indian-style raised house was built in 1799, on the banks of Bayou St. John. Once a working plantation, it was carefully moved in the 1960s a block upstream to this location. In 1810, the house

↓ Gazing out at the peaceful waters of Bayou St. John at sunset

was purchased by James Pitot, who had been the second mayor of the city five years earlier. He had arrived from Haiti in 1796 after the slave uprising led by Toussaint L'Ouverture. Pitot went on to direct a bank and run the New Orleans Navigation Company before being appointed a probate judge of the Territory of Orleans.

In 1904, Pitot House was bought by Mother Cabrini, who would later become America's first saint, and converted into a convent. It is now a museum containing original antiques and furnishings from the house.

9

Bayou St. John

📍 F3 🚋 Canal 🚌 46, 48, 90

The French recognized this bayou as a key strategic asset, providing access to the Gulf of Mexico via Lake Pontchartrain. As New Orleans grew, so did plantations along the bayou, and a canal was dug, linking it to the downtown, ending in Basin Street at Congo Square. The canal was eventually filled in and became a railroad. It has since been redeveloped as the Lafitte Greenway, a 2.6-mile (4-km) pedestrian path running from Basin Street up to Bayou St. John, whose grassy banks are one of the best places in the city to settle down with a picnic and watch the sun set.

DRINK

Twelve Mile Limit
This neighborhood bar has a wonderful secret – its cocktail menu designed by the owner, one of the city's best mixologists. The perfect casual spot to chill and sip a sundowner.

📍 E4
🏠 500 South Telemachus St 📞 504-488-8114

Finn McCool's Irish Pub
The city has a good number of Irish bars, but this one is a favorite among locals as it is one of the few places showing live soccer from Europe.

📍 E4 🏠 3701 Banks St
🌐 finnmccools.com

Bayou Beer Garden
Come for the beer and stay for the garden, a lovely hangout to drink and eat when the weather is in those sweet spots just before or just after summer.

📍 F4 🏠 326 North Jefferson Davis Pkwy
🌐 bayoubeergarden.com

⑩ Metairie Cemetery

📍 C2 🏠 5100 Pontchartrain Blvd 📞 486-6331 🚌 40, 46 🕐 8am–5pm daily

This is the most attractively landscaped cemetery in New Orleans, and the final resting place of many of its bluebloods. In the 19th century, the city was the premier venue for horseracing, and the Metairie Racetrack was the most famous. After the Civil War, mismanagement afforded Charles T. Howard the opportunity to take revenge on the racetrack members who had refused him admission. He purchased it in 1872 and converted it into a cemetery. The oval racecourse became the cemetery's main drive.

Many magnificent tombs are located here, and near the entrance stands the massive 85-ft- (26-m-) high Moriarty monument, which required the laying of a special railroad to bring it into the cemetery. Daniel Moriarty was a 19th-century Irish immigrant and saloonkeeper who succeeded financially but was shunned by the city's tight-knit elite for his background. He was determined to avenge his wife, Mary, and designed this tomb so that in death she could look down on all those who had snubbed her.

The tomb of legendary madam Josie Arlington bears a bas-relief of a young girl knocking on a door. Orphaned at the age of four, as a teenager Arlington worked as a prostitute to support her family with her earnings. Notorious for her temper, she once bit off half an ear and the lower lip of a rival.

A large bell from his boat *America* marks the grave of Captain Cooley, who ran several steamboats until his death in 1931. Other denizens include William C. C. Claiborne, the first governor of Louisiana, and P. B. S. Pinchback, a free man of color who became the state's only black governor in 1872–3. David C. Hennessy, a police chief who was assassinated by the New Orleans mob in 1891, also has an impressive tomb.

---

⑪   Degas House

📍 H3 🏠 2306 Esplanade Ave 🚌 48 🕐 By appointment only 🌐 degashouse.com

Calling himself "almost a son of Louisiana," Impressionist painter Edgar Degas (1834–1917) visited his uncle, Michel Musson *(p150)*, at this house from October 1872 until March 1873. Degas was charmed by America and especially New Orleans. Several important paintings evolved from his sojourn here, despite the fact that he did not venture far from the house for fear of the intense New Orleans sun affecting his eyesight. *The Cotton Buyer's Office* (1873) shows his uncle with several members of his family, including the artist's own brothers René and Achille, who both worked in the cotton business.

The Esplanade house, which dates from 1854, has Greek Revival details and cast-iron balconies. The house has been beautifully restored throughout, with gorgeous period furnishings and reproductions of Degas' work on display, and visitors are welcomed every morning for guided tours with one of Degas' descendents (reservations are required).

1873

The Musée des Beaux Arts in Pau, France, bought *The Cotton Buyer's Office*, Degas' first museum sale.

↑ A marble Angel of Grief draped over a tomb in Metairie Cemetery

---

SHOP

Tubby and Coo's Mid-City Book Shop

Truly independent bookstores are fast disappearing, but this progressive, self-described "nerdy" store is a local favorite. Local authors regularly hold readings and meet-and-greets here, so check the schedule.

📍 E3 🏠 631 North Carrollton Ave 🌐 tubbyandcoos.com

Pelican Furniture and Thrift Stores

A huge warehouse crammed with real bargains. Many items are sold secondhand from hotel stock, and there's almost always something weird and wonderful to tempt you.

📍 E3 🏠 341 North Hennessey St 📞 483-9996

↑ An alley of oaks lining the drive of Longue Vue House, and *(inset)* the pristine rear gardens and fountain

12
Cypress Grove Cemetery

📍 D3 🏠 120 City Park Ave
📞 482-0233 🚌 40, 46
🕐 8am–4:30pm daily

This cemetery, established by the Firemen's Charitable and Benevolent Association, was laid out in 1841, and the decision was made to move the remains of firemen who had been buried in other cemeteries in New Orleans and reinter them here. The impressive Egyptian-style gate leads into a graveyard filled with handsome memorials. Many of the tombs are dedicated to individual firefighters, such as Irad Ferry, who lost their lives in the line of duty. Ferry's tomb, which features a broken column, was designed by famous architect J. N. B. de Pouilly *(p114)*.

The cemetery also contains a large number of monuments to rich Protestants, who were buried here after Girod Street Cemetery began to deteriorate. Many of the tombs have remarkable ironwork, such as the weeping cupid gate, which is crowned with lovebirds and set between inverted torches. Other residents include several former mayors, plus theatrical impresario and entrepreneur James H. Caldwell, who built the first English-language theater in New Orleans.

An extension to Cypress Grove was built right across the street to fulfil a need for space after the yellow fever epidemic of 1853. Known as Greenwood Cemetery, it was the first in New Orleans to be built without a boundary wall. It is the site of the city's first Civil War Memorial.

13
Longue Vue House and Gardens

📍 B3 🏠 7 Bamboo Rd 🚌 34, 39 🕐 10am–5pm Mon-Sat, 1–5pm Sun 🚫 Public hols
🌐 longuevue.com

Cotton broker Edgar Stern and his wife Edith Rosenwald, heiress to the Sears fortune, built this estate between 1939 and 1942. When the couple finally moved into their new home, the sizable alley of oaks that line the drive was already established, made possible by installing 20-year-old live oaks rather than saplings. The lavish interiors are decorated with antiques, carpets, and fine art, including works by Jean Arp, Pablo Picasso, and Barbara Hepworth. The gardens, which contain no fewer than 23 fountains, created by Ellen Biddle, are exceptional examples of landscape design. The largest garden is modeled on the 14th-century Alhambra Gardens in Spain; others are inspired by French and English designs. Designed for younger visitors, the Discovery Garden is an educational and interactive half-acre environment for children of all ages.

A SHORT WALK
CITY PARK

Distance 1.1 miles (1.8 km) **Time** 20 minutes
Nearest Streetcar Canal

This 1,300-acre park is among the ten largest urban parks in the U.S. Hurricane Katrina caused damage to the grounds, trees, infrastructure, and facilities, but most of the park has reopened and is thriving. Visitors flock to the spectacular Botanical Garden and the New Orleans Museum of Art, while Storyland, a theme park with rides and fairy tale exhibits, is a great spot for kids. Eight miles (12 km) of lagoons allow for fishing and boating, and ancient trees amid lush planting grant ample dappled shade for picnics.

Storyland and Carousel Gardens *are the main attractions in the amusement park (p170).*

The landscaped **Goldring/Woldenberg Great Lawn** *hosts many concerts and events.*

VICTORY AVENUE

DREYFOUS DRIVE

CITY PARK AVENUE

Did You Know?

The vast City Park is 50 percent larger than Central Park in New York City.

Situated beside a pretty lagoon, **the Peristyle** *has been a popular gathering spot for more than a century.*

Playgrounds surround **Popp's Bandstand**, *which is named after lumber magnate John Popp.*

Strolling in the cool shade of the Dueling Oaks

Locator Map
For more detail see p164

City Park
MID-CITY

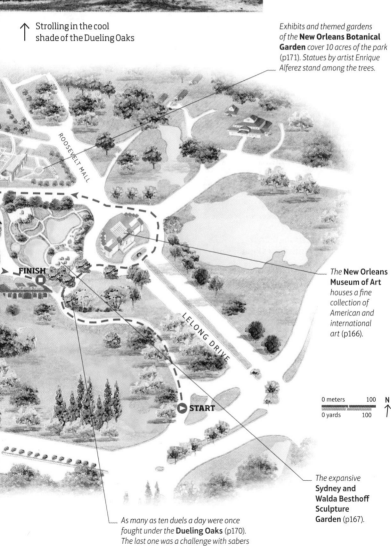

Exhibits and themed gardens of the **New Orleans Botanical Garden** *cover 10 acres of the park (p171). Statues by artist Enrique Alferez stand among the trees.*

ROOSEVELT MALL

LELONG DRIVE

FINISH

START

The **New Orleans Museum of Art** *houses a fine collection of American and international art (p166).*

The expansive **Sydney and Walda Besthoff Sculpture Garden** *(p167).*

As many as ten duels a day were once fought under the **Dueling Oaks** *(p170). The last one was a challenge with sabers that took place in 1939.*

0 meters 100
0 yards 100
N

A LONG WALK
FAUBOURG ST. JOHN

Distance 2 miles (3.2 km) **Time** 40 minutes
Nearest Streetcar Canal Streetcar

This walk circles a portion of Bayou St. John, the natural waterway that drains into Lake Pontchartrain, visited by kayakers, picnickers, and the occasional pelican. The bayou is a historically strategic waterway, where some of the city's earliest colonial development took place: it is surrounded by original Creole mansions and the distinctive above-ground St. Louis Cemetery #3. The area is easily accessible from downtown via the Canal streetcar and is not far from the attractions in City Park *(p176)*.

Locator Map
For more detail see p164

Begin this walk at North Carrollton Avenue. Cross Esplanade Avenue bridge and follow the grassy footpath around **Bayou St. John** *(p173).*

↑ Pitot House, built for the third mayor of New Orleans, James Pitot

You'll soon reach **Pitot House**, *an outstanding example of the Creole architecture built in this area in the 18th and early 19th centuries (p173).*

Beside Pitot House is the private **Cabrini High School**, *named for America's first canonized saint, Mother Frances Cabrini who established an orphanage here in 1905.*

A steel pedestrian bridge by the school takes you across the water to the grassy opposite bank of the bayou.

At the next bridge at **Dumaine Street** *cross back to the west side of the bayou, where embankments and steps provide good spots to sit and admire the wildlife and views.*

Did You Know?

Invasive Asian swamp eels have made the bayou their home, but how they got there is a mystery.

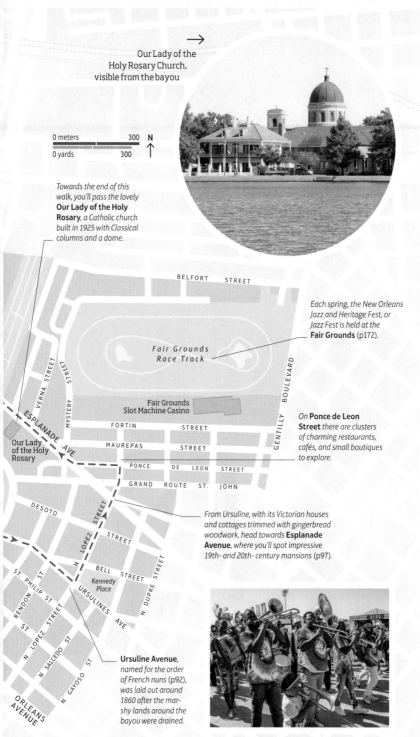

Our Lady of the
Holy Rosary Church,
visible from the bayou

0 meters 300 N
0 yards 300

Towards the end of this
walk, you'll pass the lovely
**Our Lady of the Holy
Rosary**, a Catholic church
built in 1925 with Classical
columns and a dome.

BELFORT STREET

Each spring, the New Orleans
Jazz and Heritage Fest, or
Jazz Fest is held at the
Fair Grounds (p172).

Fair Grounds
Race Track

VERNA STREET
MYSTERY STREET

ESPLANADE AVE

Our Lady
of the Holy
Rosary

GENTILLY BOULEVARD

Fair Grounds
Slot Machine Casino

FORTIN STREET

MAUREPAS STREET

PONCE DE LEON STREET

GRAND ROUTE ST. JOHN

On **Ponce de Leon
Street** there are clusters
of charming restaurants,
cafés, and small boutiques
to explore.

DESOTO

LOPEZ STREET

STREET

BELL STREET

N DUPRE STREET

Kennedy
Place

URSULINES AVE

ST. PHILIP ST

RENDON ST

N LOPEZ STREET

N SALCEDO ST

N GAYOSO ST

ORLEANS
AVENUE

From Ursuline, with its Victorian houses
and cottages trimmed with gingerbread
woodwork, head towards **Esplanade
Avenue**, where you'll spot impressive
19th- and 20th- century mansions (p97).

Ursuline Avenue,
named for the order
of French nuns (p92),
was laid out around
1860 after the mar-
shy lands around the
bayou were drained.

↑ Free Spirits Brass Band playing
at Jazz Fest in the Fair Grounds

BEYOND NEW ORLEANS

In the countyside surrounding New Orleans, the Mississippi meanders west through marsh and swampland. This is where the Acadians arrived from Nova Scotia in 1764, to settle around the bayous and prairies now known as Cajun Country. Today, towns such as Lafayette, Opelousas, and Eunice showcase the region's rich Cajun history and culture.

Baton Rouge lies north west of New Orleans. Today an oil-refining center, the city was established as a French fort in 1719. Following a century of secession and seizure, it became the Louisiana state capital in 1849. In the 18th and 19th centuries, the fertile river banks from New Orleans to Baton Rouge were lined with hundreds of plantations, where cash crops like sugarcane and indigo were cultivated to be shipped around the world. By 1850, two-thirds of America's millionaires lived in vast mansions along this stretch, the River Road, along with the thousands of enslaved people who worked and resided on the plantations. Today, some of the antebellum mansions that remain have been revitalized as museums. The Whitney is a particularly poignant example – its tours and exhibits explore the experience of life on the plantation, from the perspective of the enslaved.

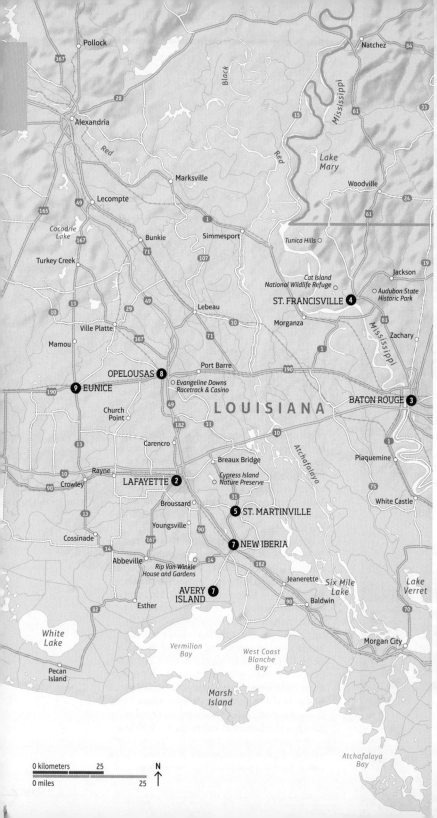

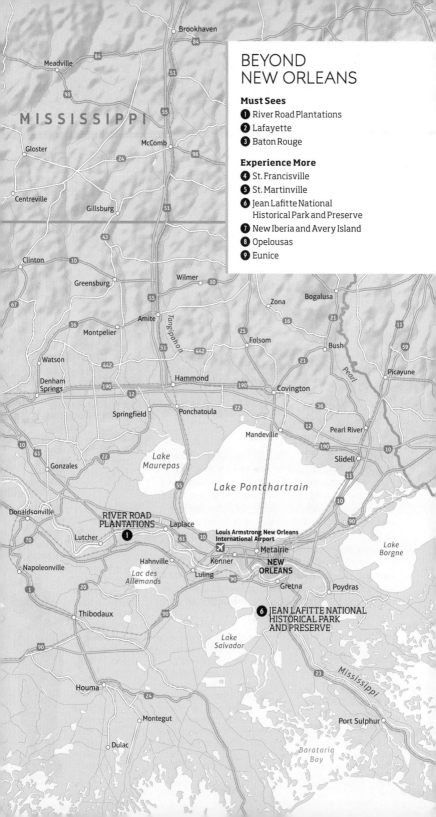

BEYOND
NEW ORLEANS

Must Sees
1 River Road Plantations
2 Lafayette
3 Baton Rouge

Experience More
4 St. Francisville
5 St. Martinville
6 Jean Lafitte National Historical Park and Preserve
7 New Iberia and Avery Island
8 Opelousas
9 Eunice

MISSISSIPPI

Brookhaven

Meadville

Gloster

McComb

Centreville

Gillsburg

Clinton

Greensburg

Wilmer

Zona

Bogalusa

Montpelier

Amite

Folsom

Bush

Watson

Denham Springs

Hammond

Covington

Picayune

Springfield

Ponchatoula

Mandeville

Pearl River

Slidell

Lake Maurepas

Gonzales

Lake Pontchartrain

Donaldsonville

RIVER ROAD PLANTATIONS
1

Laplace

Louis Armstrong New Orleans International Airport

Lake Borgne

Lutcher

Hahnville

Kenner

Metairie

NEW ORLEANS

Napoleonville

Lac des Allemands

Luling

Gretna

Poydras

Thibodaux

6 JEAN LAFITTE NATIONAL HISTORICAL PARK AND PRESERVE

Houma

Lake Salvador

Mississippi

Montegut

Port Sulphur

Dulac

Barataria Bay

Tangipahoa

Pearl

❶

RIVER ROAD PLANTATIONS

⌂ 50 miles (80 km) NW of New Orleans

The River Road is a 70-mile (130-km) corridor that follows the Mississippi River towards Baton Rouge. In the 1850s, hundreds of antebellum mansions lined this stretch, owned by wealthy planters who profited from trading sugarcane, a cash crop processed by a captive labor force of thousands of enslaved people. Today, the road meanders past petrochemical plants and surviving plantation houses, a few still surrounded by slave quarters and sugar mills. Some of these residences have been given a new lease on life as small museums, where visitors can learn about Louisiana's plantation history and the enslaved people who once lived here.

> **INSIDER TIP**
> **Plantation Tours**
>
> At the Whitney, the only museum to focus mostly on the perspective of those enslaved, guided walking tours of the site offer a unique insight into plantation life. Tours last 90 minutes, and should be booked in advance.

① ⚐ Ⓜ

The Whitney Plantation

⌂ 5099 Louisiana Hwy 18, Edgard ⏰ 9:30am-4:30pm Wed-Mon
🌐 whitneyplantation.com

Located near Wallace in St. John the Baptist Parish, the Whitney Plantation Historic District stretches across some 2,000 acres and is now an exceptional museum dedicated to those enslaved at the plantation. The original plantation dates back to 1752, though the main part of the house, built in a French-Creole raised style, was built in 1803. Curated by a Senegalese historian specializing in the history of the slave trade, the museum opened its doors in 2014 after some 15 years of preparation.

Visitors can read the oral histories of some of the last survivors of slavery, recorded by the Federal Writers Project in the 1920s, and see Woodrow Nash's sculptures of these last survivors, who were children at the time of emancipation.

→
Sculpture of a formerly enslaved young girl at the Whitney Plantation

↑ The tunnel of trees leading to Oak Alley plantation house

There are poignant memorials listing names of the people enslaved here, and specially commissioned works of art. Original slave cabins and many of the outbuildings still survive.

Oak Alley

🏠 3645 Hwy 18, Vacherie
🕐 Opening hours vary, check website 🌐 oak alleyplantation.com

Oak Alley's name comes from the 28 live oaks that line the entrance to this former sugar plantation. They were planted over 300 years ago, before the house was built by enslaved laborers for Creole planter Jacques Telesphore Roman III in 1837. Oak Alley was established as a sugarcane plantation, but pecans were also harvested here: Antoine, an enslaved gardener, developed the first commercial variety of pecan nut, the "Paper Shell," on the property.

There are exhibits on the process of sugar production and slavery, and visitors can wander the plantation's striking main house and grounds, which have been used as the location for several movies.

Laura

🏠 2247 Hwy 18, Vacherie
🕐 10am–4pm daily
🔒 Public hols 🌐 laura plantation.com

Revolutionary War veteran Guillame Duparc was given a large land grant, and built this French Creole plantation house in 1805. After he died, four generations of women ran the sugar plantation.

Laura gained notoriety for the stories told by the French-speaking enslaved people, later tenant farmers, living there. Folklorist Alcée Fortier first translated these Senegalese stories of folk hero Brer Rabbit.

Guided tours of the main house and surviving outbuildings explore the history of the plantation. A permanent exhibition is dedicated to telling the story of the enslaved community who lived and worked at this Creole farm.

GRINDING SEASON

Processing sugarcane, the primary crop grown along the River Road, was a brutal endeavour. In the early 19th century, grinding season (from mid-October) saw enslaved workers toil around the clock to harvest the mature canes. The canes were ground in sugar mills, and the resulting pulp boiled in huge sugar kettles known as "Jamaica Trains." The labor was relentless and conditions perilous – workers sustained machete wounds while harvesting in the dark, and terrible burns while cooking the sugar over an open flame, and fatalities were common.

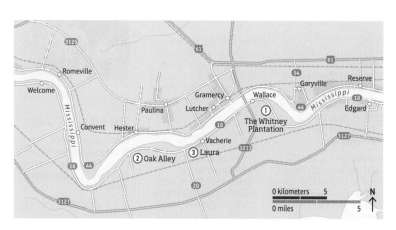

② LAFAYETTE

⌂ 135 miles (217 km) W of New Orleans ✈ 2 miles (3.2 km) SE 🚌 100 Lee Avenue 🛈 1400 NW Evangeline Throughway; lafayettetravel.com

When the first Acadians arrived in this area, they settled along the bayous and in the prairies west of New Orleans. These rural people, also known as Cajuns, worked as farmers and made a living from the swamps. Lafayette is now Cajun Country's largest city. Community centers, restaurants, several detailed reconstructions of Cajun villages, and a distinct local architectural style have imprinted this city with a truly unique atmosphere.

① Lafayette Museum/Alexandre Mouton House

⌂ 1122 Lafayette St
🕐 10am–4pm Tue–Sat
🚫 Public hols 🖥 lafayettemuseum.com

Jean Mouton, founder of Lafayette, built the original house around 1800. He, his wife Marie, and their 12 children used it only on Sundays when they came from their plantation in Carencro to attend church and socialize. In 1825, the sixth son, Alexandre, moved his family and law practice into the house. He later became a United States senator and governor of Louisiana – a notable example of Cajun success. The house contains furnishings, paintings, maps, and documents relating to the city's history, plus some glittering Mardi Gras costumes and regalia.

THE ACADIANS

Driven by the British from Acadia in Nova Scotia, Canada, French-Canadian Acadians (or "Cajuns") settled in Louisiana from 1764. Disparaged for generations, the Arcadians have survived numerous threats to their Francophone culture. Today, their distinctive Cajun cuisine and music is highly acclaimed.

② The Acadian Village

⌂ 200 Greenleaf Dr
🕐 10am–4pm Mon–Sat
🚫 Jan 1, Thanksgiving, Dec 25, Mardi Gras 🖥 acadianvillage.org

At this version of a re-created 19th-century Cajun village,

Did You Know?

Today, Cajun Country is the largest French-speaking community in the United States.

←

Traditional Cajun buildings at the Acadian Village, a living history museum in Lafayette

most of the buildings are original, although they have been moved here from other locations. The houses are furnished with typical Cajun furniture and tools, and are tended by costumed guides who demonstrate a variety of traditional skills such as spinning, weaving, and blacksmithing.

③

Acadian Cultural Center

🏠 501 Fisher Rd
🕐 Opening hours vary, check website 🌐 nps.gov

The informative exhibits of photographs and artifacts here focus on Acadian culture,

including language, music, architecture, religion, cuisine, the Cajun Mardi Gras, and handicrafts. A film dramatizes the British deportation of the Acadian population from Canada, charting their diaspora to France and to places along the east coast of North America, before their final arrival in Louisiana.

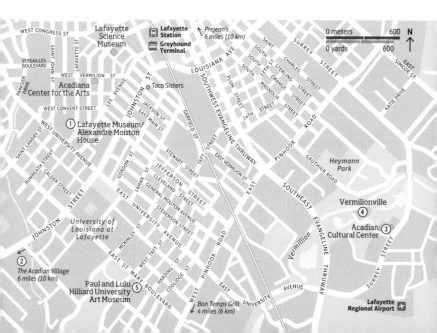

↑ A craftsperson using a wheel to spin cotton at Vermilionville, a living re-creation of Cajun life

Vermilionville

◪300 Fisher Rd
🕙10am-4pm Tue-Sun (last admission 3pm) 🚫Public hols ⓦvermilionville.org

This fascinating living-history museum features a collection of buildings dating from 1790 to 1890 assembled into a typical Cajun village over 23 acres (9.3 hectares). Its name, Vermilionville, was the original name for the city of Lafayette. Costumed artisans demonstrate the skills that were needed to survive in 18th- and 19th-century Louisiana: woodworking, blacksmithing, spinning, weaving, and cooking. Wandering from building to building, visitors can imagine what traditional Cajun life was like. A performance hall, where Cajun bands regularly entertain, is open in the afternoon.

INSIDER TIP
Special Sausage

You can't leave Cajun Country without tasting the *boudin,* a regional specialty sausage made from pork blood and rice. Look out for tasty variations like deep-fried *boudin* balls, or different fillings, from shrimp and crawfish, to alligator.

Paul and Lulu Hilliard University Art Museum

◪1710 E St. Mary Blvd
🕙9am-5pm Tue-Fri (to 8pm Thu), 10am-5pm Sat 🚫Public hols ⓦhilliardmuseum.org

This small art museum is located on the campus of the University of Louisiana at Lafayette. The museum was founded in 1968 and has a permanent collection of more than 1,500 works including paintings, sculpture, folk art, and textiles. The emphasis is on the cultural heritage of Louisiana. The museum is housed in a modern glass and steel building with state-of-the-art exhibition spaces. Its many outstanding works of art include European and American art from the 18th, 19th, and 20th centuries, 2nd century BC Egyptian artifacts, and a superb collection of African American folk art. Diverse architectural drawings, as well as student works, are displayed along with temporary exhibits all year long.

MUSIC IN CAJUN COUNTRY

Cajuns have a strong musical tradition, rooted in the folk music that the French-Canadian settlers brought with them in the 19th century. Cajun music's catchy dance numbers and soulful ballads are closely related to Zydeco music, which you'll also hear a lot of in Louisiana.

CAJUN MUSIC

As the Acadians traveled to the South they brought what musical instruments they could carry, and kept their folk music alive. Down in Louisiana, they were influenced by Jamaican and Haitian sounds, and European accordion music. Styles of Cajun music range from traditional (with lively accordian, fiddle, and triangle playing), through Texas swing (with piano and swung rhythms), to contemporary (rock and R&B influenced), but all forms of Cajun music are catchy and up-tempo.

ZYDECO MUSIC

Zydeco shares many elements with Cajun music, but is known as the music of Louisiana Creoles. Zydeco combines traditional R&B, blues, jazz, gospel, and Cajun dance music, and features call and response patterns from African folk music. Fast tempo Zydeco dance pieces incorporate the accordian, guitar, drums and fiddle, along with the *vest froittoir* or Zydeco rubboard – a percussion instrument made from corrugated steel.

↑ Dancing the Cajun two-step

→ Accordian player Anthony Dopsie performing

CAJUN DANCE PARTIES

At traditional Cajun dance parties, or *fais do-dos*, dancehall Cajun music is performed to accompany two-step, the Cajun Jitterbug and the waltz (three-step). Literally translating as "go to sleep," the phrase *fais do-do* would have been said to children who would sleep while their parents danced the night away.

↑ Zydeco musician Geno Delafose entertaining dancers in Breaux Bridge

3

BATON ROUGE

🏠 90 miles (144 km) NW of New Orleans ✈ 9430 Jackie Cochran Drive 🚌 Greyhound Bus Lines, 1001 Loyola Ave
ℹ 359 Third Street; www.visitbatonrouge.com

In 1719, the French established Baton Rouge as a fort designed to control access to the Mississippi and the interior. In 1762, the French ceded it to the British. During the American Revolution, the Spanish seized the garrison, which remained under their control until 1810 when the local American population proclaimed it the Republic of West Florida. The area was incorporated into the Union in 1817 and has been the state capital since 1849.

①

Louisiana State University

🏠 Nicholson Drive between Highland Rd and W Chimes St 🌐 lsu.edu

With its 31,000 students, the LSU is the state's flagship university. The campus is attractively landscaped and has some unique features. In the northwest corner, for example, two mounds rise some 20 ft (6 m) high. Archaeologists believe that they are 5,000-year-old American Indian ceremonial mounds, the oldest in the country, built even before the first Egyptian pyramids.

The university has two cutting-edge research facilities: the Pennington Biomedical Research Center, devoted to nutritional medicine; and the Center for Microstructures and Devices. The collection at the Museum of Natural Science in Foster Hall is also worth seeing. The visitor information center is at Dalrymple Drive and Highland Road.

Louisiana State's sports team games are some of the hottest tickets in college sports. In baseball, the Tigers have won national titles for several consecutive years, and the enthusiasm generated by the football team is legendary.

②

Old Governor's Mansion

🏠 502 North Blvd ⏰ By tour hourly 10am–4pm Tue–Fri (last tour 3pm) 🔒 Public hols 🌐 oldgovernorsmansion.org

Louisiana Governor Huey Long had this mansion built in 1930. He modeled it on the White House, even down to the office, which is a smaller version of the Oval Office. The building has been

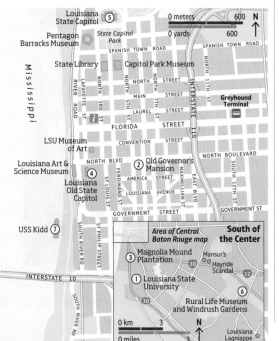

DRINK

Hayride Scandal
Opened in 2017, this classy cocktail joint has the air of a seasoned speakeasy, with plush decor and a well-stocked bar. The perfect spot to sip whiskey and bourbon craft cocktails and enjoy a taste of Southern hospitality.

🏠 5110 Corporate Blvd 🌐 hayridescandal.com

→

The winding staircase of the Old State Capitol's rotunda, and *(inset)* its fortress-like exterior

carefully restored, and the rooms have even been repainted in their original colors, some of which are outlandish; Huey Long apparently loved hot pinks, purples, and greens, which appear in several bathrooms. Many of the furnishings in the library and the master bedroom are original to the house. There is also memorabilia from other governors, including the singing governor Jimmie Davis, who wrote the famous song *You Are my Sunshine*.

Magnolia Mound Plantation

🏠 2161 Nicholson Dr
🕐 10am-4pm Mon-Sat,
1-4pm Sun ⏰ Public hols
🌐 brec.org/magnolia
mound

John Joyce had this plantation home built in 1791. In the 19th century, it stood at the center of a 900-acre farm, where crops, including tobacco and sugarcane, were cultivated by enslaved workers until the 1860s. Purchased by the City of Baton Rouge in 1966, the building has been carefully

restored to reflect the antebellum era. The main house holds a small museum, and visitors can explore the former slave quarters and open-hearth kitchen.

Louisiana Old State Capitol

🏠 100 North Blvd 🕐 9am-4pm Tue-Fri, 9am-3pm Sat ⏰ Public hols 🌐 louisiana oldstatecapitol.org

James Harrison Dakin designed this striking castle-like building in 1847. William Freret conceived the soaring iron spiral staircase, installed during a renovation in 1882, which winds from the foyer toward the stained-glass dome. In 1861, it was here, in the House Chamber, that Louisiana's state representatives voted to secede from the Union. Seven decades later, in 1929, impeachment proceedings were begun here against Huey "Kingfish" Long. Today, this magnificent building serves as the state's Center for Political and Governmental History. Visitors can view and listen to the state's political orators expressing their views.

> In 1861, it was here, in the Old State Capitol's House Chamber, that Louisiana's state representatives voted to secede from the Union.

HIDDEN GEM
Highland Park Road Observatory

On the southern edge of Baton Rouge, just a 20-minute drive from the city center, this lovely observatory (run by the LSU) hosts scientific lectures and sky viewings (www.bro.lsu.edu).

⑤

Louisiana State Capitol

🏛 State Capitol Dr at N 3rd St 📞 (225) 342-7317
🕐 8am–4:30pm daily
🚫 Jan 1, Easter Sunday, Thanksgiving, Dec 25

The 40th Louisiana Governor Huey Long worked hard to persuade legislators to approve the \$5 million funding for this Modernist 34-story building, erected in 1932. It is the tallest capitol in the United States. Both the House and Senate chambers are impressive, as are the murals in Memorial Hall.

Still visible are the bullet holes in the marble walls of the first-floor executive corridor, where Long was assassinated on September 8, 1935, by Dr. Carl A. Weiss, the son-in-law of a political enemy, Judge Benjamin Pavy.

The grounds of the Capitol are home to Long's grave in a sunken memorial garden, presided over by a statue of the governor.

Visitors can enjoy excellent views of the Mississippi river and the city from the Capitol's 27th-floor observation deck.

⑥

Rural Life Museum and Windrush Gardens

🏛 4560 Essen Lane at I-10 🕐 8am–5pm daily
🚫 Jan 1, Easter Sunday, Thanksgiving, Dec 24 & 25

Ione Burden and her brother, Steele, who landscaped Louisiana State University, assembled this collection of buildings and 19th-century tools and artifacts. Each building is filled with fascinating objects, including a washing machine dating from 1900, pirogues (a type of boat used on the bayous), and a tobacco press. Steele Burden's paintings and ceramic figures are also displayed, along with other collectibles. Steele also rescued all the buildings from nearby Welham Plantation and re-erected them in a typical plantation layout. Here, exhibits and restored plantation buildings provide an insight into how such a plantation functioned as a self-contained community.

⑦

USS Kidd

🏛 305 S River Rd
🕐 9:30am–3:30pm Mon–Fri, 10am–4pm Sat & Sun
🚫 Thanksgiving, Dec 25
🌐 usskidd.com

Commissioned in 1943, this World War II destroyer saw action in the Pacific, where it suffered a kamikaze attack on April 11, 1945, and 38 of the crew were killed.
The ship also deployed in the Korean War and other missions until 1964, when it was decommissioned. Guided tours explore the cramped quarters shared by the 330-man crew below decks, and visitors can view the anti-aircraft guns. There is even the option for small parties to stay the night and camp on board the ship.

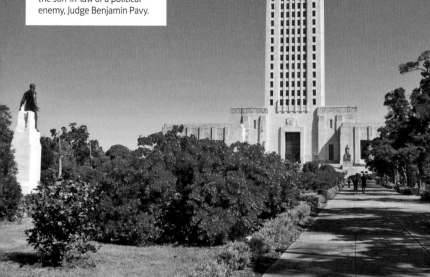

EAT

Mansur's

At this sophisticated restaurant, one of the city's few upscale options for Creole dining, seafood features heavily on the menu. The shrimp and grits dish is an exercise in decadence.

🏠 5720 Corporate Blvd A
🌐 mansursonthe
boulevard.com

⑤⑤⑤

Louisiana Lagniappe

Seafood specialists who vow only to serve crawfish, crab, and oysters in season. A house favorite is the gulf fish stuffed with shrimp and topped with crab, served *en papillote*.

🏠 9990 Perkins Rd
🌐 louisianalagniappe
restaurant.com

⑤⑤⑤

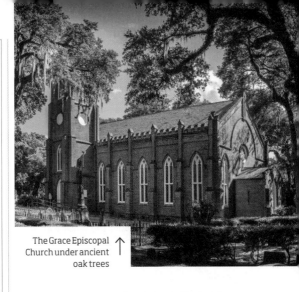

The Grace Episcopal Church under ancient oak trees ↑

The towering Louisiana State Capitol, the seat of the state's government

EXPERIENCE MORE

 4

St. Francisville

🏠 112 miles (180 km) NW of New Orleans 🛈 West Feliciana Tourist Office, 11757 Ferdinand St; www. stfrancisville.us

Dating back to 1809, the secluded St. Francisville has long been known as "the town two miles long and two yards wide," due to its location on a narrow ridge overlooking the Mississippi. In the early 19th century, it was an important port and briefly served as the capital of the Republic of West Florida. Today, the town has a population of less than 2,000, but many of the buildings put up during the town's heyday survive, and it is popular with daytrippers from New Orleans.

The historic downtown has several 19th-century churches, the oldest of which is the **Grace Episcopal Church** (1827). The **West Feliciana Historical Society Museum** is likewise housed in a 19th-century building and covers the cultural and architectural history of the area. A few minutes away, **Audubon State Historic Site** was where

famous ornithologist John James Audubon spent much of his time *(p157)*. Explore the great outdoors at the **Cat Island National Wildlife Refuge**, host to many species in its wetland habitats, or hike and camp in the vast forests of **Tunica Hills**.

Grace Episcopal Church

🏠 11621 Ferdinand St
🌐 gracechurchwfp.org

West Feliciana Historical Society Museum

🏛 🏠 11757 Ferdinand St
🕐 9am–5pm daily
🌐 westfelicianahistory.org

Audubon State Historic Site

♿ 🕐 🏠 11788 LA-965
🕐 9am–5pm Wed–Sun
🌐 crt.state.la.us

Cat Island National Wildlife Refuge

🕐 Seasonally 🛈 West Feliciana Tourist Office; 11757 Ferdinand St 🌐 fws. gov/refuge/cat_island

Tunica Hills

🏠 LA-66, St Francisville
🌐 wlf.louisiana.gov/ wma/2752

St. Martinville

📍 138 miles (222 km) NW of New Orleans 🛈 215 Evangeline Blvd; www.stmartinville.org

This small picturesque town on a natural levee of the Bayou Teche was founded in 1765 as a military outpost. It became known as "Petit Paris" after many French noblemen settled here having fled the French Revolution. In the main square the **Acadian Memorial** houses *The Arrival of the Acadians in Louisiana*, a mural by Robert Dafford, who modeled some of the portraits on contemporary descendants. Opposite the painting, the Wall of Names lists some 3,000 early Acadians. Behind the museum, an eternal flame burns in a courtyard garden above Bayou Teche.

Nearby the Evangeline Oak marks the spot where the two famous Acadian lovers, Gabriel and Evangeline, of poet Henry Wadsworth Longfellow's epic *Evangeline, A Tale of Acadie*, supposedly met.

Established in 1765 by French missionaries, **St. Martin de Tours Church** was the first church to serve the Acadian community. While fairly plain inside, it contains a baptismal font that was a gift from Louis XVI, and a replica of the grotto at Lourdes. The grave of Evangeline Labiche (mythologized in Longfellow's *Evangeline*) and a bronze statue of her are located in the garden behind the church. The monument was donated by actress Dolores del Río, who played the role of Evangeline in the silent movie filmed here in 1929. Stretched along Bayou Teche, the **Longfellow-Evangeline State Historic Site** offers picnicking and walking trails among 300-

year-old oaks. At the center of the park stands a reconstruction of a typical Acadian cabin from the 1790s. There is also a museum, which focuses on Acadian history and culture.

A 15-minute drive from St. Martinville is Lake Martin, set between Lafayette and Breaux Bridge, where the **Cypress Island Nature Preserve** is a stunning example of Louisiana swampland. Stands of moss-veiled cypress trees overlook waters home to alligators, turles, snakes, and water birds. There is a boardwalk and visitor's center at the south side of the lake.

Acadian Memorial
♿ 📍 121 S New Market St ☎ (337) 394-2258 🚫 Public hols

St. Martin de Tours Church
📍 133 S Main St ⏰ 8am-6pm daily 🌐 stmartindetours.org

Longfellow-Evangeline State Historic Site
♿ 📍 1200 N Main St ⏰ 9am-5pm Wed-Sun 🌐 crt.state.la.us

Cypress Island Nature Preserve
📍 1264 Prairie Hwy, St. Martinville 🌐 nature.org

Jean Lafitte National Historical Park and Preserve

📍 6588 Barataria Blvd, Marrero 🌐 nps.gov

In the early 19th century, legend has it that the pirate Jean Lafitte used the lands around here to hide treasure. Whatever the truth to that, this national historic park is well worth hunting down. This section of the park opened in 1978, incorporating the existing Barataria Preserve into the network of sites. The park has a total of six sites across the state, but this one in Marrero covers about 20,000 acres of

→

Snowy rows of egrets nesting amid the verdant plant life of Avery Island bayous, forests, and swamps. The nature trails offer the chance to see a wealth of local wildlife, from alligators and beaver-like nutria to over 300 bird species. There's an informative visitor's center with exhibits on the ecological significance of the wetlands and there impact on Louisiana culture. There are also special Junior Ranger activities for children as well as guided tours.

New Iberia and Avery Island

🏠 133 miles (214 km) W of New Orleans 🚌 1103 E Main St 🛈 2513 Highway 14; www.cityofnewiberia.com

New Iberia is notable for its many sugarcane plantations. The area also owes its wealth to salt mining. In fact, the so-called "islands" here, such as Avery and Jefferson, are domes sitting atop salt mines.

At the plantation home known as **Shadows on the Teche**, a cache of 17,000 letters, photographs, receipts, and papers relating to the plantation owners and enslaved workers that lived here was found. This is used as back-

720
—
Drops of Tabasco® hot sauce fill each bottle of of Avery Island's classic spicy condiment.

ground for the fascinating tour of the house.

The **McIlhenny Company Tabasco Factory and Jungle Gardens** on Avery Island is the source of the famous condiment, an essential ingredient in Bloody Marys and in local cuisine. Some 75 acres of pepper plants blaze red here from August to November, and visitors can tour the factory. The founder considered himself a botanist-naturalist and the Jungle Gardens that he assembled are spectacular. In addition to abundant exotic plant life, the gardens also shelter a diverse population of egrets, herons, and peacocks, as well as nutria. Wildfowl stop here in winter.

The **Rip Van Winkle House and Gardens** are located on the Jefferson Island salt dome. It was built by actor Joseph Jefferson in 1870 and named

after the role he played 4,500 times. An architectural hodge-podge of Moorish, Steamboat Gothic, and Victorian, the house is surrounded by beautiful gardens, which are on the banks of Lake Peigneur.

After Joseph Jefferson died in 1905, J. Lyle Bayless of the Salt Island Mining Company purchased the house. Shortly afterward, oil was discovered on the property. It was soon producing up to 250,000 barrels of oil a week from 30 wells. In 1972, the Texaco Oil Company mistakenly drilled through the salt dome, causing an explosion that set off a minor tidal wave on the lake. Miraculously, no one was killed.

Shadows on the Teche
♿ 🏠 317 E Main St, New Iberia ⏰ 10am–4pm Mon–Sat 🚫 Public hols 🌐 shadows ontheteche.org

McIlhenny Company Tabasco Factory and Jungle Gardens
♿ ♿ 🏠 Hwy 329, Avery Island ⏰ Factory: 9am–4pm daily; gardens: 9am–5pm daily 🚫 Public hols 🌐 tabasco.com

Rip Van Winkle House and Gardens
♿ 🏠 5505 Rip Van Winkle Rd, Jefferson Island ⏰ 9am–4pm daily 🚫 Public hols 🌐 ripvanwinklegardens.com

Moss-wreathed cypresses on Lake Martin, St. Martinsville

EAT

Soileau's Dinner Club

A second-generation Cajun restaurant famed for its oysters and shrimp. Try the crawfish if they're in season, and the gumbo any time.

📍1618 N Main St, Opelousas
🌐solieaus.com

The St. John Restaurant

This unassuming wooden building houses a surprisingly inventive kitchen that prides itself on its Cajun classics, such as frog's legs, fried alligator, and sautéed crab fingers.

📍203 N New Market St, St. Martinville 🌐the stjohnrestaurant.com

---

Opelousas

📍138 miles (222 km) NW of New Orleans ℹ828 E Landry St; www.cityof opelousas.com

The capital of Confederate Louisiana during the Civil War, and the state's third oldest city, Opelousas was named after the American Indian tribe that lived in this area before the Europeans arrived. The current city was founded as a French trading post during the 1700s, and is now one of the liveliest towns in this district, thanks to its cuisine and music.

Opelousas is the ideal place to explore on foot, with clusters of antebellum, Victorian, and early-20th-century build-

↑ Trees lining Court Street in the center of the historic old town of Opelousas

ings spread around town. The major collections of the **Opelousas Museum and Interpretive Center** focus on local culture and history. The museum's two main exhibit areas are devoted to the prehistory of the area, its agricultural and commercial development, and the people of different races and religions who have contributed to the region's culture. One room is devoted to Civil War memorabilia, while another houses a collection of more than 400 dolls. The museum also houses the Louisiana Video Library and the archives of the Southwest Louisiana Zydeco Festival.

A slice of Opelousas life is on view at **Le Vieux Village**, a historical park and museum with a collection of buildings from the 1700s, including a church, a schoolhouse, and a doctor's office, that offers visitors an opportunity to appreciate the historic local architecture. A tourist information center is also located here, as well as a small museum devoted to native son Jim Bowie, who was the hero of the Alamo and the namesake of the well-known frontier knife.

The **Evangeline Downs Racetrack & Casino** is a state-of-the-art facility offering both quarter-horse and thoroughbred racing (on separate dates). It is cheerily referred to as a "racino" – that is, a racetrack with a full casino component,

which is a growing institution among US racetracks.

Opelousas Museum and Interpretive Center

♿ 📍315 N Main St 📞(337) 948-2589 🕐8am-4:30pm Mon-Fri 🚫Public hols

Le Vieux Village

♿ 📍28 E Landry St 📞(337) 948-6263 🕐10am-2pm Tue-Fri 🚫Public hols

Evangeline Downs Racetrack & Casino

♿ 📍2235 Creswell Lane Extension 🕐Opening hours vary, check website 🌐evangeline downs.com

---

Eunice

📍158 miles (254 km) NW of New Orleans 🚌1238 W Landry St ℹ200 South CC Duson Dr; www.eunice-la.com

Every weekend is a celebration of Cajun music in this picturesque Louisiana town, where most of the main attractions are downtown. The town was founded in 1893 by C. C. Duson, who named it in honor of his wife. The **Liberty Theater** is the keeper of the flame of Cajun music – the Grand Ole Opry of Cajun music. It opened in the 1920s as a movie and vaudeville theater. Every

Saturday from 6pm to 8pm, it hosts a live broadcast of the *Rendez-Vous des Cajuns* radio show, filled with Cajun and zydeco music and plenty of good Cajun humor. The master of ceremonies makes introductions in both English and French.

Visitors to the **Prairie Acadian Cultural Center**, just behind the theater, can observe musical instruments being made in the craft room. Other displays highlight aspects of Acadian culture, including the *Courir*. Literally "to run," this is the Cajun, and distinctly medieval, version of Mardi Gras. Participants wear a *capuchon* (a tall, cone-shaped hat, which covers the face as well as the head) and ride on horseback from farm to farm begging for the ingredients for a community gumbo, which will be eaten at the end of the day. The key ingredient, the chicken, has to be chased down and caught live.

Located nearby are two other cultural centers. The **Cajun Music Hall of Fame and Museum**, which opened in 1997, honors the originators of Cajun music and the artists who have kept the tradition alive. It displays memorabilia, instruments, photos, and biographies of the 80 or so inductees.

> **Other displays highlight aspects of Acadian culture, including the *Courir*. Literally "to run," this is the Cajun, and distinctly medieval, version of Mardi Gras.**

Cajun music is a blend of several different traditions – German, Scottish, Irish, Spanish, Afro-Caribbean, and American Indian – which have been laid over a base of French and French-Acadian folk tradition. Zydeco developed from the same traditions but incorporates more Afro-Caribbean rhythms and styles.

The Hall of Fame features many great names in Cajun music, from early legends such as Amédé Ardoin, Alphé Bergeron, Dennis McGee, Joe Falcon, Amédé Breaux, Iry Lejeune, and Lawrence Walker, to more recent adopters, such as Michael Doucet, Zachary Richard, and Wayne Toups.

On the way from Eunice to Opelousas along Highway 190, the **Savoy Music Center** is the informal headquarters for Cajun musicians and fans in the area. The store is owned by accordion-maker-musician Marc Savoy and his wife, Ann. It sells musical instruments, records, and books on Cajun culture and music. On Saturday mornings, local musicians assemble in the front of the store for a jam session around the upright piano. They bring their fiddles, accordions, and triangles, and strike up together in a spontaneous, rousing spectacle. You're welcome to bring your own beer, boudin, and snacks, and join in with the celebrations.

Liberty Theater
♿ 🏠 200 Park Ave 📞 (337) 457-7389 🕐 4pm Sat

Prairie Acadian Cultural Center
🏠 250 W Park Ave 📞 (337) 457-8499 🕐 8am-5pm Tue-Fri, 8am-6pm Sat 🔒 25 Dec

Cajun Music Hall of Fame and Museum
🏠 240 South CC Duson Dr 📞 (337) 457-6534 🕐 Summer: 9am-5pm Tue-Sat; winter: 8:30am-4:30pm Tue-Sat 🔒 Public hols

Savoy Music Center
🏠 Hwy 190 East, Savoy 📞 (337) 457-9563 🕐 9am-noon & 1:30-5pm Tue-Fri, 9am-noon Sat 🔒 Public hols

↑ Musicians at the grave site of legendary Cajun fiddler Dennis McGee

NEED TO KNOW

Streetcars on the Canal Street Line

BEFORE YOU GO

Forward planning is essential to any successful trip. Be prepared for all eventualities by considering the following points before you travel.

AT A GLANCE

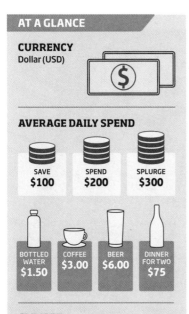

CURRENCY
Dollar (USD)

AVERAGE DAILY SPEND

SAVE	SPEND	SPLURGE
$100	$200	$300

BOTTLED WATER	COFFEE	BEER	DINNER FOR TWO
$1.50	$3.00	$6.00	$75

CLIMATE

 The longest days occur from June to August, and the shortest from October to April.

 Temperatures average 80° F (26° C) in summer and drop below 50° F (10° C) in winter.

 June has the heaviest rainfall. Hurricane season is from June to November.

ELECTRICITY SUPPLY

The standard U.S. electric current is 110 volts and 60 Hz. Power sockets are type A and B, fitting plugs with two flat pins.

Passports and Visas

Canadian and Mexican visitors require a valid passport to enter the U.S. Citizens of Australia, New Zealand, and the EU do not need a visa, but must apply to enter in advance for the Electronic System for Travel Authorization (**ESTA**) and have a valid passport. All other visitors will need a passport and tourist visa to enter, and will be photographed and have their fingerprints checked. A return airline ticket is required to enter the U.S. Be sure to allow plenty of time for the U.S. border agency's thorough passport and visa checks at the airport. Entry regulations may change, so check in advance of travel with the U.S. Department of State *(below)* for the most up-to-date visa and travel information.
ESTA
ⓦ esta.cbp.dhs.gov/esta.

Travel Safety Advice

Visitors can get up-to-date travel safety information from the **U.S. Department of State**, the **UK Foreign and Commonwealth Office**, and the **Australian Department of Foreign Affairs and Trade**. The **National Hurricane Center** has a useful page for hurricane information and safety precautions.
Australia
ⓦ smartraveller.gov.au
National Hurricane Center
ⓦ nhc.noaa.gov
UK
ⓦ gov.uk/foreign-travel-advice
U.S. Department of State
ⓦ travel.state.gov

Customs Information

Passengers may carry the following into the U.S. without incurring tax:
Tobacco products A carton of cigarettes, 50 cigars or two kilograms (4.4 lbs) of smoking tobacco.
Alcohol A liter of alcohol as beer, wine or liquor (if aged 21 years or older); $100 in gifts.
Cash If you are carrying $10,000 or more in cash

you must declare it to the customs authorities. Nonresident travelers need to complete a **Customs and Border Protection Agency** form when crossing the U.S. border.
Customs and Border Protection Agency
cbp.gov/travel

Insurance

Emergency medical insurance is highly recommended for international travelers to the U.S., as costs for medical and dental care can be high. Travel insurance for cancellations, delays, theft, and loss of belongings is recommended. Car rental agencies offer vehicle and liability insurance; check your policy before traveling.

Vaccinations

No inoculations are required for visiting the United States.

Money

Most establishments accept major credit, debit, and prepaid currency cards. Contactless payments are becoming increasingly common, but cash is usually required by smaller shops and businesses, street vendors, and on buses. ATMs are available at nearly every bank and street corner.

Booking Accommodations

With around 38,000 hotel rooms available, New Orleans offers a good choice of accommodations. The city's top hotels can be expensive, but there are also many budget and mid-priced hotels, family-run B&Bs, and hostels. Hotels are busiest mid-week when business travelers are in the city, and during major festivals such as Mardi Gras. Rates are subject to an additional 13 percent room tax, plus a $1-2 room fee per night.

Travelers with Specific Needs

Ramps, elevators, and special parking spaces can be found around the city. However, few of the historic buildings have these facilities, nor do most restaurants and bars. Always enquire about mobility restrictions in advance of visiting.

Outside of the French Quarter and Downtown areas, sidewalks may be in a state of disrepair and not suitable for wheelchairs. On public transport, both the Canal and Riverfront streetcar routes and all RTA buses have wheelchair ramps.

The **Advocacy Center** provides advice and services for people with specific needs in the state of Louisiana.
Advocacy Center
advocacyla.org

Language

New Orleans is a cosmopolitan city in which you will hear multiple languages spoken, and Louisiana's rich cultural heritage means that French, Spanish, Cajun, Creole, German, and American Indian words have been mixed together into a New Orleans patois (p220).

Many tour companies cater for those with limited English with foreign language headsets and guided tours in a range of languages.

Closures

Mondays and Tuesdays Museums and many restaurants close on Mondays or Tuesdays.
Sundays Most banks are closed and many smaller businesses close for the day.
Federal and State Holidays Museums, attractions and many businesses close, especially for major holidays. It is best to check with individual venues for specific closures ahead of your visit.

FEDERAL HOLIDAYS

1 Jan	New Year's Day
3rd Mon in Jan	Martin Luther King, Jr. Day
3rd Mon in Feb	President's Day
Last Mon in May	Memorial Day
4 July	Independence Day
2 Sep	Labor Day
28 Nov	Thanksgiving Day
25 Dec	Christmas Day

GETTING AROUND

Whether exploring New Orleans on foot or by public transportation, here is all you'll need to navigate the city like a pro.

PUBLIC TRANSPORT COSTS

SINGLE BUS OR STREETCAR JOURNEY

$1.25
(plus 25 cents to transfer)

ONE DAY JAZZY PASS

$3
Unlimited bus and streetcar journeys

FIVE DAY JAZZY PASS

$15
Unlimited bus and streetcar journeys

SPEED LIMIT

RURAL FREEWAYS
70 mph
113km/h

URBAN FREEWAYS
60 mph
(96km/h)

URBAN AREAS
30 mph
(48km/h)

NEIGHBORHOOD SLOW ZONE
20 mph
(32km/h)

Arriving by Air

Located about 15 miles (24 km) from downtown New Orleans, the **Louis Armstrong International Airport** is the city's main airport. All the major U.S. airlines, including American Airlines, Southwest Airlines, United Airlines, and Delta Air Lines, have scheduled services to Louis Armstrong International Airport. Most of them also service international flights, but these will usually entail a connection at another U.S. airport en route. Air Canada offers scheduled flights direct from Toronto to New Orleans, while American Airlines, Delta, and United all operate from the United Kingdom. British Airways has a direct route from London Heathrow.
Louis Armstrong International Airport
W flymsy.com

Domestic Train Travel

Amtrak, the U.S. passenger rail service, offers routes to New Orleans from a number of cities across the country. Visitors traveling to New Orleans by train arrive at Amtrak's Union Passenger Terminal on Loyola Avenue, at the edge of the Central Business District (CBD), near the Superdome. Noted for their comfort and luxury, all long-distance Amtrak trains have a full complement of refreshment facilities and sleeping accommodations. At peak times, passengers are advised to reserve seats in advance on many services. Amtrak offers a range of special deals and packages, including 5-, 15-, and 30-day passes that allow unlimited travel. Note that these are available only for international travelers.
Amtrak
W amtrack.com

Long-Distance Bus Travel

Long-distance coach services are operated by **Greyhound Bus Lines** and arrive at Union Passenger Terminal. This terminal, which is shared with Amtrak, provides full baggage, ticketing, and package express services throughout the day and into the early hours

GETTING TO AND FROM THE AIRPORT

Airport	Transport	Price	Journey time
Louis Armstrong International Airport	Airport shuttle	$24	30 minutes
	Taxi	$36	25 minutes
	City Bus (202)	$1.50	45 minutes

of the morning. Greyhound buses are modern, clean, and safe. Some services are express, with few stops between major destinations, while others serve a greater number of cities. If you are planning to break your journey several times along the way, or you wish to tour the country, there are various packages designed to suit your requirements. Overseas visitors should also note that passes may be less expensive if you buy them from a Greyhound agent outside the U.S.

Greyhound Bus Lines
w greyhound.com

Public Transportation

Although most of the city's popular tourist sights in and near the French Quarter are easily accessible on foot, the New Orleans Regional Transport Authority (**RTA**) runs an efficient public transportation system. Bus routes crisscross the city, but no visitor should miss the opportunity to travel on the oldest streetcar in the nation – St. Charles Streetcar (p142). Ferries are a pleasant way to cross and travel along the Mississippi River.

RTA
w norta.com

Planning Your Journey
Buses are busiest during the rush hours: 7–9am and 4.30–6pm. Streetcars can be packed throughout the day, and are especially busy during major festivals such as Mardi Gras and Jazz Fest. Note that public transportation runs a reduced service during major holidays. The RTA's GoMobile smartphone app provides live transport information.

Tickets
The RTA offers one-way and express fares as well as a variety of pass options (Jazzy Pass) for the bus, streetcar, and ferry network. Jazzy Passes are available as 1-, 3-, 5-, and 31-day

passes. They can be purchased online from the RTA website and GoMobile app, or from various vendors across New Orleans, such as the ticket vending machines along the Canal Streetcar line. Fares and passes are only applicable on the New Orleans RTA system.

On buses, streetcars, and ferries, one-way tickets and one-day passes can be purchased directly from your bus driver or a streetcar operator, with cash only.

Bus
Bus stops are indicated by white and yellow signs displaying the RTA logo. The route numbers of the buses stopping there are usually listed at the bottom of the sign. Buses stop only at designated bus stops, which are located every two or three blocks, depending on the area of the city.

Buses in New Orleans are less frequent and less reliable than in many major U.S. cities, so be sure to check schedules, especially outside of peak hours. All New Orleans buses are accessible to travelers with specific needs, and guide dogs are allowed on board. Front seats are reserved for senior citizens and disabled passengers. Buses have bike racks that can accommodate up to two bicycles on board.

On boarding the bus, put the exact change or number of tokens in the fare box, or show your Jazzy Pass to the driver. Smoking, drinking, eating, and playing music are all prohibited on buses.

Ferries
The **Canal Street Ferry** (RTA) crosses the river daily, carrying pedestrians and vehicles from the Central Business District to Algiers Point, on the West Bank. The ferry departs every 30 minutes from around 6am to 9:30pm daily.

Canal Street Ferry
w norta.com/Maps-Schedules/ New-Orleans-Ferry

Streetcar

New Orleans' streetcars makes a pleasant way to get around the city, moving at a moderate pace and stopping frequently around major sights. There are five streetcar lines in New Orleans, all operated by the RTA.

The Riverfront Streetcar line travels a distance of 2 miles (3 km) along the Mississippi Riverfront, from Esplanade Avenue, at the far side of the French Quarter, to the New Orleans Convention Center in the CBD. The streetcar runs approximately every 20 minutes from 7:10am to 10:30pm during the week, and from 8:40am to 10:30pm on weekends.

The first stop for the St. Charles Streetcar is at the corner of Canal and Carondelet streets. The streetcar turns onto Canal Street, then back around on St. Charles Avenue for the trip uptown. It travels the length of St. Charles Avenue, turning on to Carrollton Avenue at the Riverbend, and terminating at Claiborne Avenue. The return trip is the reverse of the outbound trip until Lee Circle, where it turns onto Carondelet Street to get to Canal Street. This line operates 24 hours a day and runs every 7 minutes, but is less frequent off peak.

The Canal Streetcar route starts at the Riverfront, at the foot of Canal Street, and runs to City Park Avenue. There is also a spur line along North Carrollton Avenue, linking Canal Street to the New Orleans Museum of Art and City Park at Beauregard Circle. It runs approximately every 30 minutes from 7am to 2am.

The Rampart–St. Claude Streetcar line runs from Canal Street to Elysian Fields Avenue along Rampart Street and St. Claude Avenue. This line operates between approximately 6am to midnight, and runs every 15 minutes.

When you board the streetcar, pay the driver in cash (with the exact fare) or swipe your Jazzy Pass. You will need to pull the cord to indicate that you want to disembark. You can exit from either the front of the car or the back, depending on how crowded the streetcar is. Each streetcar displays its destination on the front.

Bus Tours

One of the most popular ways to see the sights is aboard a hop-on-hop-off bus tour. Get off wherever you like, and catch another bus when you are ready. **Hop-On Hop-Off** offers such tours aboard double-decker buses.

Hop-On Hop-Off
ⓦ hop-on-hop-off-bus.com

Taxis

The city's taxis are affordable, convenient, and highly recommended for trips after dark to areas outside the French Quarter. Cabs are easily found at airports, bus and train stations, all major hotels, and regular taxi stands. For time-sensitive journeys, pre-book a taxi; **United Cabs** is recommended. Arrange a pickup at a definite time and place. All fares should be metered according to the distance traveled. All taxis have a light on their windshield to indicate when they are available. **Uber** also operates in New Orleans.

Uber
ⓦ uber.com
United Cabs
ⓒ (504) 522-9771
ⓦ unitedcabs.com

Driving

The good public transportation network and short distances between sights make driving in central New Orleans largely unnecessary, but a car is convenient if you wish to visit the surrounding countryside, or nearby Louisiana cities of Baton Rouge and Lafayette.

Driving in the city takes patience, good skills, good humor, and the ability to read the road and the street signs quickly. In central New Orleans, be prepared for heavy traffic and a severe shortage of parking facilities, especially in the French Quarter.

New Orleans is notorious for large potholes; drive carefully and make sure there is paved road ahead. Frequent heavy downpours can cause street flooding. Make sure to drive slowly through standing water, or if possible find another route.

Car Rental

Rental car companies are located at the airport and other locations in the city. To rent a car in the U.S. you must be at least 25 years old with a valid driving license and a clean record. All agencies require a major credit card.

Damage and liability insurance is recommended just in case something unexpected should happen. It is advisable always to return the car with a full tank of gas; otherwise you will be required to pay the inflated fuel prices charged by the rental agencies. Be sure to check for any pre-existing damage to the car and note this on your contract before you leave the rental lot.

Parking

If you do decide to drive in the city, check with your hotel to see if they offer parking; this will usually add at least $25 per night to your bill. Otherwise, there are meters across the city, charging $3 per hour in the French Quarter, CBD and Warehouse District, and $2 per hour elsewhere. Meters do not have to be paid between 7pm and 8am, or on Sundays. Use the

ParkMobile app to avoid having to return to your car every one or two hours to feed the meter; a parking fine will set you back $30. Avoid parking in the French Quarter, where the narrow streets are frequently cleaned, meaning that cars must be moved or face being towed away (see street signs). Parking on any major city street or thoroughfare is forbidden during Mardi Gras. The city's tow-away crew is very active.

ParkMobile
ⓦ parkmobile.io

Rules of the Road

All drivers are legally required to carry a valid driver's license and must be able to produce registration and insurance documents. Most foreign licenses are valid, but if your license is not in English, or does not have a photo ID, apply for an International Driving Permit.

Seat belts must be worn in cabs at all times, and in private vehicles, seat belts are compulsory in front seats and are suggested in the back. Children under 3 years old must ride in a child seat in the back.

Traffic drives on the right-hand side of the road, and the speed limit is usually 35 mph (56 km/h) unless otherwise stated. When it is safe to do so you may turn right on a red light. If a school bus stops to let passengers off, all traffic from both sides must stop and wait for the bus to drive off.

Drinking and Driving

A limit of 0.08 percent blood alcohol is strictly enforced at all times. For drivers under the age of 21 there is a zero tolerance policy for drink-driving – driving while intoxicated is a punishable offense that incurs heavy fines or even a jail sentence.

Breakdown Assistance

In the event of an accident or breakdown, drivers of rental cars should contact their car rental company first. Members of the American Automobile Association (**AAA**) can have their vehicle towed to the nearest service station to be fixed. For simple problems like a flat tire or a dead battery, the AAA will fix it or install a new battery on site for a fee.

AAA
ⓦ aaa.com

Walking

The city is made up of distinct neighborhoods and it is often simplest to take public transportation to a particular area and then explore on foot. The French Quarter, for example, is particularly compact and easily strolled around. A variety of guided and unguided walking tours are available. **Friends of the Cabildo** conduct daily tours of the historic French Quarter. Tours start outside the 1850 House at 10:30am and 1:30pm. Tickets can be reserved online in advance. **Two Chicks Walking Tours** lead groups around the French Quarter, Garden District, and the city's cemeteries, with tours focusing on quirky and unexpected aspects of history.

Wear comfortable shoes; some sidewalks and streets in New Orleans are very old and uneven. Parts of Mid-City, Uptown, and the Bywater are best avoided at night, but it is wise to be cautious at all times in all areas of New Orleans.

Friends of the Cabildo
ⓦ friendsofthecabildo.org
Two Chicks Walking Tours
ⓦ twochickswalkingtours.com

Cycling

Cycling in New Orleans is easy and convenient thanks to the city's flat, gridded network of streets, and bike-friendly initiatives. It's a leisurely way to see the city and experience the charm of its historic neighborhoods. All city buses are equipped with bike racks, allowing you to combine modes of transport. Be sure to lock your bike securely when you park it, as bicycle thefts are common. **Bicycle Michael's** and **FreeWheelin' Bike Tours** offer rental services, as well as guided tours. The city's bike sharing scheme, **Blue Bikes**, has stations around the city. It can be used by registering online and then paying with a credit card.

The **Lafitte Greenway** is a 2.6-mile- (4-km-) long pedestrian and cycle trail. A pleasant, tree-lined stretch, the Greenway links Armstrong Park to City Park, where there are more cycle paths to explore.

Bicycle Michael's
ⓦ bicyclemichaels.com
Blue Bikes
ⓦ bluebikesnola.com
FreeWheelin' Bike Tours
ⓦ neworleansbiketour.com
Lafitte Greenway
ⓦ lafittegreenway.org

Boats Trips

Traditional riverboats offer tours stopping at popular destinations. The *Creole Queen* runs two cruises: a day trip to the Chalmette Battlefield, where the Battle of New Orleans took place, and a night cruise that includes dinner accompanied by live jazz. The **Steamboat** *Natchez* (p74) offers a two-hour tour in the morning and a night cruise with an excellent buffet and live jazz.

Creole Queen
ⓦ creolequeen.com
Steamboat *Natchez*
ⓦ steamboatnatchez.com

PRACTICAL
INFORMATION

A little local know-how goes a long way in New Orleans. Here you will find all the essential advice and information you will need during your stay.

EMERGENCY NUMBERS

GENERAL EMERGENCY

911

TIME ZONE
CST/CDT (Central Daylight Time)
PST +3
UTC/GMT -6
AEDT +15

TAP WATER
Unless otherwise stated, tap water in New Orleans is safe to drink.

TIPPING

Waiter	15-20%
Bartender	$1 per drink
Hotel Porter	$2 per bag
Housekeeping	$5 per day
Cab Driver	10-15%

Personal Security

As in any city, there are parts of New Orleans that may not be especially tourist friendly. Visitors should be alert in all areas, but anyone who takes precautions should enjoy a trouble-free trip. Plan routes in advance, look at maps discreetly, and walk with confidence. If you need directions, ask hotel or shop staff, or the police. Stay in a large group when sightseeing outside the French Quarter (especially after dark), and do not challenge a thief. If you have anything stolen, report the crime within 24 hours to the nearest police station and take ID with you. Get a copy of the crime report in order to claim on your insurance. Contact your embassy if you have your passport stolen, or in the event of a serious crime or accident.

Health

It is possible to visit a doctor or dentist in New Orleans without being registered, but you will be asked to pay in advance. Keep receipts to make a claim on your insurance later. There are plenty of walk-in medical clinics, emergency rooms, and 24-hour pharmacies. **CrescentCare** offers convenient walk-in or by-appointment services at locations around the city. Hospital emergency treatment is available 24 hours a day. If you are able, call the number on your insurance policy first, and check which hospitals your insurance company deals with. For emergency treatment, call an ambulance. Payment medical expenses is the patient's responsibility. Arrange comprehensive medical insurance before traveling.
CrescentCare
W crescentcarehealth.org

Smoking, Alcohol, and Drugs

Smoking is prohibited in all public buildings, bars, restaurants, and stores. Cigarettes can be purchased by those over 18 years old; proof of age will be required.

The legal minimum age for drinking alcohol in the U.S. is 21, and you will need photo ID as proof of age in order to purchase alcohol and be

allowed into bars. In New Orleans, it is legal to drink alcohol in public (in a can or plastic container) but it is illegal to carry an open container of alcohol in your car, and penalties for driving under the influence of alcohol are severe.

Possession of illegal drugs is prohibited and could result in a prison sentence.

ID

It is not compulsory to carry ID at all times in New Orleans. If you are asked by police to show your ID, a photocopy of your passport photo page (and visa if applicable) should suffice. You may be asked to present the original document within 12 or 24 hours.

Local Customs

You may walk around with alcoholic drinks bought in bars, but transfer them to a plastic cup (go-cup) before you leave the bar and finish your drink before you enter another bar. Wearing Mardi Gras beads outside of Mardi Gras season marks you as a tourist and may invite attention from pickpockets or muggers.

Visiting Churches, Cathedrals, and Synagogues

Dress respectfully: cover your torso and upper arms, and ensure shorts or skirts cover your knees.

Cell Phones and Wi-Fi

Cafés and restaurants will usually permit the use of their Wi-Fi on the condition that you make a purchase.

Cell phone service in New Orleans is generally excellent but if you are visiting from overseas and want to guarantee that your cell phone will work, make sure you have a quad-band phone. In order to use your phone abroad you may need to activate the "roaming" facility. Other options include buying a prepaid cell phone in the U.S. or a SIM chip for a U.S. carrier.

Mail

Stamps can be purchased from post offices and drugstores. On-street mailboxes are usually blue, and are for letters only. Small packages must be taken to a post office. The city's main **General Post Office** is open from 9am to 5pm Monday to Friday. It can take from one to five days to arrive at its destination.
General Post Office
w usps.com

Taxes and Refunds

Taxes will be added to hotel and restaurant charges, theater tickets, some grocery and store sales, and most other purchases. Always check if tax is included in the price displayed. Sales tax is around 9 percent, and hotel tax is around 16 percent.

When tipping in a restaurant, it is the norm to include tax in your calculation. A quick way to calculate restaurant tips is simply to double the tax, which adds up to 18 percent. Tax-free shopping is available to foreign visitors who are staying in the U.S. for fewer than 90 days at participating stores.

Discount Cards

New Orleans Pass offers a number of visitor passes and discount cards for exhibitions, events, museum entry, and even transportation. These are available online and from participating tourist offices. The cards are not free; consider how many of the offers you are likely to take advantage of before purchasing.
New Orleans Pass
w neworleanspass.com

WEBSITES AND APPS

New Orleans
Visit the city's official tourist information website at *www.neworleans.com*.

NORTA GoMobile App
New Orleans' RTA public transport app for tracking streetcars, buses, and ferries in real time, at *www.norta.com/ Getting-Around/NEW-GoMobile*.

Mardi Gras Parade Tracker
The best app for information about the dozens of carnival parades, at *www.mardigrasparadetracker.com*.

PHRASE BOOK

South Louisiana has a rich heritage of blending its disparate cultures, and New Orleans is no exception. French, Spanish, Cajun French, Creole French, English, German, and some American Indian words have all been mixed together into a New Orleans patois. The following is a list of the most frequently used words and phrases, plus a guide to correct pronunciation.

WORDS AND PHRASES

armoire	(arm-wah) **cupboard or wardrobe**
arpent	**measure of 180 ft (55 m)**
au dit	(oh-dee) **ditto or "the same"**
aw-right	**accepted greeting or acclamation on meeting friend s or acquaintances**
banquette	(ban-ket) **sidewalk**
baptiser	(bap-tee-zay) **to give a name to something**
bateau	**boat**
bayou	(bay-you or bye'o) **a waterway or creek**
boeuf	(berf) **cow, meat, steak**
Boureé	**Cajun card game**
bousillage	(boor-sill-arge) **mixture of Spanish moss and mud, used to insulate walls**
brulé	(bru-lay) **burned, toasted (as in café brulé)**
cabinette	**outhouse**
cocodrie	**alligator**
Cajun	**descendants of the Acadians who settled in South Louisiana in the 18th century**
charivari	(shi-va-ree) **noisy mock serenade to a newly married older couple**
chaudron	**a cauldron or large kettle**
cher	(share) **widespread term of endearment in Cajun French**
cold drink	**soda with ice**
coulée	(cool-ay) **ravine or gully**
Creole	**descendant of original French or Spanish settlers**
Creole of color	**descendant of French or Spanish settlers with African blood**
doubloons	**aluminum coins thrown to Mardi Gras crowds**
dressin' room	**polite term for the bathroom**
fais-do-do	(fay-doh-doh) **literally "go to sleep"; Cajun term for a community dance where parents bring their children, who often fall asleep to the music**
fourche	**the fork of a creek (as in Bayou Lafourche)**

gallery	**balcony or porch**
gris-gris	(gree-gree) **voodoo charm**
Guignolée	**New Year's Eve celebration**
jour de l'An	**New Year's Day**
krewe	**private club that sponsors a parade and a ball during Mardi Gras**
lagniappe	(lan-yap) **"something extra" at no cost**
levee	**embankment for flood control or riverside landing**
neutral ground	**the median of a large avenue or street (the St. Charles Avenue streetcar runs on the neutral ground)**
nonc	**uncle**
nutria	**South American rodent imported to Louisiana in the late 18th century. The nutria is an important part of the fur industry**
ouaouaron	(wah-wah-rohn) **bullfrog**
parish	**civil and political division in Louisiana (like a county)**
patois	(pat-wah) **dialect: different Cajun communities speak their own patois**
pirogue	(pee-row) **long, shallow canoe**
praline	(praw-LEEN) **candy made with sugar, cream, and pecans, very popular in New Orleans**
rat de bois	(rat-de-bwah) **opossum**
shotgun house	**long, narrow house**
T or Ti	**petite, junior, a nickname (T-frere = baby brother)**
Vieux Carré	(voo-cah-RAY) **literally "Old Square", the French Quarter**
ward	**political division of New Orleans**
where y'at?	**how are you?**

STREET AND TOWN NAMES

Atchafalaya	(chaf-fly) **large (800,000 acres) swampy wilderness area in South Louisiana**
Tchoupitoulas St	(chop-a-TOOL-us)
Burgundy St.	(bur-GUN-dy)
Chartres St.	(CHART-ers)
Euterpe St.	(YOU-terp)

Melpomene Ave.	(MEL-pom-meen)		gumbo	spicy soup with okra, tomatoes, seafood, served over rice
Metairie	(MET'ry) **suburb of New Orleans**		jambalaya	thick stew of rice, sausage, seafood, vegetables, and spices
Terpsichore St.	(TERP-si-core)			
Opelousas Ave.	(opp-a-LOO-sas)		muffuletta	huge sandwich of cold cuts, cheese, and olive salad, served on Italian bread
Lafayette	(laugh-e-YET) **unofficial capital of Cajun Country**			
Plaquemine	(PLACK-a-meen) **town and parish south of Baton Rouge**		okra	pod vegetable, usually served in gumbo
Baton Rouge	(bat'n ROOZH) **capital of Louisiana**		oysters Rockefeller	oysters on the half shell, covered with a creamy spinach sauce, and baked on a bed of salt
Thibodeaux	(TIBB-a-doh) **common surname, also a town in Cajun Country**			
			po'boy	sandwich of fried seafood, roast beef, ham, or a mixture, served on French bread
Natchitoches	(NACK-uh-dish) **oldest town in the Louisiana Purchase area**			
Ponchatoula	(ponch-a TOOL-ah) **town on the north shore of Lake Pontchartrain**		remoulade	spicy mayonnaise-based seafood sauce
			roux	mixture of butter and flour, mixed with water and seasonings; used as a base formany soups, gravies, and sauces

CAJUN AND CREOLE COOKING

andouille	pork and garlic sausage			
beignet	square, deep-fried doughnut, dusted with powdered sugar		shrimp Creole	shrimp cooked with tomato sauce and seasoned with onions, green pepper, celery, and garlic
boudin	spicy pork, rice, and onion sausage			
bread pudding	French bread soaked in milk and egg, baked, and served with whiskey sauce		Tabasco®	hot, red pepper sauce made only at Avery Island; often used for any brand of pepper sauce, of which there are hundreds available
bouillabaisse	French seafood stew			
café au lait	dark roast coffee served with steamed milk		tasso	local highly seasoned smoked ham
chicory	coffee additive, made of roasted, ground roots			
crawfish	(cray-fish) **often called "mudbugs," a delicious, small, lobster-like crustacean found in the creeks and bayous in Louisiana**			
dirty rice	rice mixed with chicken gizzards and livers, green pepper, onions, and spices			
etouffée	method of cooking crawfish or shrimp, simmered with vegetables			
filé	ground sassafras leaves, used to thicken gumbo			
grillades	meat smothered with thick tomato gravy, always served with grits			
grits	ground, hulled corn, cooked with butter, salt, and pepper			

ACKNOWLEDGMENTS

The publisher would like to thank the following for their kind permission to reproduce their photographs:

Key: a-above; b-below/bottom; c-centre; f-far; l-left; r-right; t-top

123RF.com: Fotoluminate 100-1t; Imagecom 16c, 58-9; Andrei Ivanov 33clb; Michael Rosebrock 8cla.

4Corners: Jordan Banks 56-7; Massimo Borchi 68-9b, 70-1t.

akg-images: National Gallery of Art, Washington / *Chief of the Taensa Indians Receiving La Salle March 20, 1682* (1847/1848) by George Catlin 49tl.

Alamy Stock Photo: A.F. ARCHIVE 110clb, 116bl; Irene Abdou 171t; Rubens Alarcon 49tr, 79b; 91cra, 98b, 103tl, 177tl, 178cl; American Photo Archive 126bc; Archive Images 50-1t; Andriy Blokhin 8cl; Kristina Blokhin 80bl; age fotostock / Massimo Borchi 83tl, 90-1b; Michael Brooks 158bl; Ron S Buskirk 99br; Cavan / Joseph De Sciose 29br; Charles O. Cecil 153br, 154-5b; Naum Chayer 75cra; Patrick Civello 151b; Jeff Compasso 175cla; Cosmo Condina North America 82bl; Ian Dagnall 77bl; Danita Delimont / Adam Jones 18bl, 138-7, / Cindy Miller Hopkins 101br, / Jamie & Judy Wild 114b; dbimages / Jeremy Graham 30-1b,112-3b, / Roy Johnson 24-5t, 28cb; Beth Dixson 13br; Sean Drakes 115t; Richard Ellis 199b; Everyday Artistry Photography 91tr, 175t; FineArt 51clb; Adam Gasson 17t, 86-7; GJGK Photography 39crb; Glasshouse Images / Circa Images 52cr; Tim Graham 17bl, 104-5, 154tr, 188tl; Granger Historical Picture Archive 50tl,110bc; Leigh Green 113tl; Steve Hamblin 101cr, 126cb; hemis.fr / Patrick Frilet 137tr, 186crb, 189b; Ian Dagnall Commercial Collection 198tr; Images-USA 96cla, 109br, 160bl, / *Statue of Louis Armstrong "Satchmo"* by Elizabteh Catlett © Catlett Mora Family Trust / VAGA at ARS; NY and DACS; London 2019 109cra; jejim120 135cr; Inge Johnsson 174bl; Brenda Kean 19t, 162-3; Keystone Press 53clb; Daniel Korzeniewski 91tl; James Houser New Orleans 118-9t; Jason Langley 166-7b; Simon Leigh 85br, 184br; Andy Levin 91br, 173b; Melvyn Longhurst 99tl; Martin Thomas Photography 94tr; Masterpics 49cb; Ninette Maumus 10-1b, 35clb, 38tl, 76t; Nitu Mistry 113cla; Newscom / BJ Warnick 54clb; Niday Picture Library 49bl; Nikreates 146-7t, 147bl, 150tl; North Wind Picture Archives 48bc, 50cla, 51cr; PJF Military Collection 55cb; The Picture Art Collection 51br; Laura Prieto 94-5b; The Protected Art Archive 142br; Reciprocity Images 39tl, 161tr;

Golden Richard 111crb; Khristina Ripak 22t; RM USA 114crb, 153cr; robertharding 128br, / Ken Gillham 153crb; Stephen Saks Photography 159tl, 194-5b; Philip Scalia 96t; Pete Titmuss 38br; Trinity Mirror / Mirrorpix 110cra; UPI / A.J. Sisco 189crb; Francis Vachon 48crb; Vespasian 100br; Jim West 46cl, 171cla; Jennifer Wright 130bl, 132bl, 151crb; ZUMA Press; Inc. 80-1t, / Daniel DeSlover 8clb.

Audubon Nature Institute: 40-1t, 125tl, 125tr, 131t, 131cra, 144-5t, 145cra, 145clb, 145br; Digital Roux Photography LLC 124-5b, / Susan Poag 125cra.

AWL Images: Patrick Frilet 12-3b; Marco Gaiotti 196-7; Christian Heeb 10ca; Jason Langley 18tr, 24tl, 120-1, 152-3t.

Bella Blue: Roy Guste 45bl.

Blue Bikes New Orleans: 35tr.

Bridgeman Images: Davis Museum and Cultural Center, Wellesley College, MA, USA - Museum purchase with funds provided by Wellesley College Friends of Art *Storyville Portrait, c.1912* (gelatin silver printing-out print) by E. J. Bellocq 52br; Granger / *1803 American cartoon, c. 1900, on the purchase of Louisiana by the United States from France* 50clb.

Brustman Carrino Public Relations: Hot Tin / Randy Schmidt 10clb, / Sienna Viette 25tl.

Catahoula Hotel: Sarah Essex Bradley 33tr.

Cochon - Link Restaurant Group: Chris Granger 137br.

Contemporary Arts Center: Ryan Hodgson-Rigsbee / *Casa das Canoas [Rio]. 2013* by Sarah Morris 136br.

© DACS 2019: *Statue of Louis Armstrong "Satchmo"* by Elizabteh Catlett / © Catlett Mora Family Trust / VAGA at ARS, NY and DACS, London 2019 109cra; *Untitled,1991, Bronze, ed. 4 / 4* by Joel Shapiro © ARS, NY and DACS, London 2019 New Orleans Museum of Art purchase, Sydney and Walda Besthoff Foundation Fund, 98.213 167t.

Dorling Kindersley: William Reavell 27tr; Helena Smith 179tr.

Dreamstime.com: Joe Benning 172-3t; F11photo 42-3b; Fotoluminate 156-7t; Roberto Galan 4; Wangkun Jia 55br; Legacy1995 149tr; Maomaotou 132t, 161br; Meinzahn 12clb, 143; Sean Pavone 6-7, 52-3t, 63, 184-5t, 200-1;

Photofires 62c;Anne Power 46cla; Terryfultineer 81cla; Lawrence Weslowski Jr 85tl.

The Ehrhardt Group - Compère Lapin: Dominique Ellis 26b.

French Quarter Festival, Inc presented by Chevron: Zac Smith 47tr.

Getty Images: 500Px Unreleased Plus / Steve Tosterud 93br; AFP 55t; Archive Photos / Charles Peterson 110-1t, / P. L. Sperr 142cb; Bettmann 43tl, 51tr; Bloomberg 39tr; Canopy / Robert Mullan 100crb; Cavan Images 34tr; Christian Science Monitor 43cl, 54cr; AWL Images / John Coletti 108-9t; John Coletti 25cla; Corbis Documentary / Atlantide Phototravel 126-7, 167cra, 168-9t, / VCG / Robert Holmes 102bl; Corbis Historical / Stefano Bianchetti 110crb; Corbis NX / Richard T. Nowitz 116-7t; De Agostini 50br, / Biblioteca Ambrosiana 52tl; DigitalVision / Marianna Massey 24cra; FilmMagic / Josh Brasted 53br, / Erika Goldring 31tr; Cheryl Gerber 66-7b; Sean Gardner 67clb; Erika Goldring 11cr, 12t, 28-9t, 46cra, 66bc, 67cla, 67cl, 109cb,133bl, 172bl; Tim Graham 11br; Icon Sportswire 46clb; The Image Bank / Anne Rippy 192-3b; ; Tyler Kaufman 47cla, 53tr; The LIFE Picture Collection / Mansell 142clb; Lonely Planet Images 93tc, / Judy Bellah 40br, / Richard Cummins 191tl, 191tr, / Ray Laskowitz 34-5b, / Kylie McLaughlin 11t, 47cra, 97b, 101tr, / Stephen Saks 186-7t; Michael Ochs Archives 111clb; Ethan Miller 54bc, Moment Open / Gerard Plauche 157c; Tim Mosenfelder 45crb; MPI / Archive Photos 49cla; Photolibrary / Marianna Massey 20crb; Redferns / David Redfern 110br; Michael Serna 8-9b; Mario Tama 92br; Tribune News Service / MCT 29cla; Universal Images Group / Education Images 78tr, 148b, / Encyclopaedia Britannica 48t, / Marka 75t, / Photo 12 52cla; The Washington Post 36bl; WireImage / Skip Bolen 189cra; / Josh Brasted 179br, / Erika Goldring 27br.

HiHo Lounge: Nkechi Chibueze 44br.

The Historic New Orleans Collection: 72cra, 72-3b, 73tr, 73cla; *Portrait of Lydia Brown (1922–28)* by Josephine Marien -Gift of Laura Simon Nelson 73cra; Gift of Harold F. Naquet and Cheron Bryiski, 2016.0172.3.43 113br; Gift of Mr. G. William Nott, 1974.61.1 113cra.

iStockphoto.com: Geoff Eccles 193tr; Rodrigo A. Rodriguez Fuentes 27cl; grandriver 2-3, 128-9t; Jenniveve84 66cra; peeterv 44tl; Renphoto 71cb; SeanXu 62cra; wynnter 52clb.

Krewe of Armeinius: Barrett DeLong 67bl.

LeMieux Galleries: *Corner Bar* by David Lambert 37cl.

Louisiana State Museum: Jay Rosenblatt 65clb; Mark J Sindler 64bl, 64-5t, 65crb, 65bl, 68cra.

Mardi Gras World: 41br.

Napolean House: 30tl.

NASA: image courtesy of Jeff Schmaltz, MODIS Rapid Response Team at NASA GSFC. 54crb.

Courtesy of The National WWII Museum: Jeffery Johnston 126clb.

courtesy of the New Orleans Museum of Art: 168bl, 169tr, 169crb, / *Untitled,1991, Bronze, ed. 4 / 4* by Joel Shapiro © ARS, NY and DACS, London 2019 purchase, *Sydney and Walda Besthoff Foundation Fund, 98.213* 167t, / *Looking Through the Doomsday Fog, 1990, paper maché on wood with ink notations* by Clyde Connell - Gift of Jack Sullivan in loving memory of Christopher Karnes, 2000.5.1 169cla.

New Orleans and Company: 26tl; Paul Broussard 13t, 22crb, 25tr, 46cr, 47crb; LA Gourmetreise 2010 45tl; Zac Smith 31br, 41cla, 47clb; Travelling Newlyweds 31cl.

New Orleans City Park Archives: 170br.

New Orleans Glassworks: 37br.

New Orleans Historic Voodoo Museum: Charles M. Gandolfo 113cb.

Ogden Museum of Southern Art: Ryan Hogdson / *Stormy 2015, Stoneware and acrylic paint* by Mapo Kinnord 36-7t; Ryan Hodgson-Rigsbee / *Eating Cake (2008) - Mixed media Gift of the Artist* by Shawne Major 134-5t

Picfair.com: Andrew Areoff 20cr.

Ralph's on the Park: Chris Granger 22cr.

Reuters: Jonathan Bachman 67tl.

Rex by Shutterstock: 111bc; Sipa 55bl; Startraks 46crb.

Robert Harding Picture Library: Jason Langley 13cr.

Sazerac Bar at Roosevelt Hotel / Waldorf Astoria Hotels & Resorts: Brian F Huff 32tl.

Shutterstock: Elliott Cowand Jr 92-3t; f11photo 20bl; JustPixs 22bl; Page Light Studios 112cl; Micha Weber 20t.

SuperStock: Richard Cummins 19cb, 180-1.

Tales of the Cocktail - Foxglove Communications: Cory James Photo 32-3b.

Tennessee Williams-New Orleans Literary Festival: Ride Hamilton 42tl, 47tl.

Front flap: **Alamy Stock Photo:** Adam Gasson cra; Andriy Blokhin br; **Dreamstime.com:** F11photo bl; **Getty Images:** John Coletti cla; **iStockphoto.com:** grandriver t; **Picfair.com:** Marco Montenegro.

Sheet map cover: **Picfair.com:** Marco Montenegro.

Cover
Front and Spine: **Picfair.com:** Marco Montenegro.
Back: **Dreamstime.com:** Sean Pavone cla; **Getty Images:** Lonely Planet Images / Ray Laskowitz tr; **Picfair.com:** Marco Montenegro b; **Shutterstock:** f11photo c.

For further information see:
www.dkimages.com

Penguin Random House

Main Contributers Paul Oswell, Donna Dailey, Marilyn Wood, Ian McNulty, Sarah O'Kelley, Peter Reichard, Harriet Swift
Senior Editor Ankita Awasthi Tröger
Senior Designer Tania Da Silva Gomes
Project Editor Lucy Sienkowska
Project Art Editor William Robinson
Designers Bharti Karakoti, Kitty Glavin
Factchecker Paul Oswell
Editors Matthew Grundy Haigh, Phil Hunt
Proofreader Ben Ffrancon Davies
Indexer Helen Peters
Senior Picture Researcher Ellen Root
Picture Research Sumita Khatwani, Rituraj Singh, Manpreet Kaur, Vagisha Pushp
Illustrators Ricardo Almazan, Ricardo Almazan Jr.
Senior Cartographic Editor Casper Morris
Cartography Subhashree Bharati, Ben Bowles, Rob Clyne, James Macdonald
Jacket Designers Maxine Pedliham, William Robinson
Jacket Picture Research Susie Watters
Senior DTP Designer Jason Little
DTP Rohit Rojal
Producer Samantha Cross
Managing Editor Hollie Teague
Art Director Maxine Pedliham
Publishing Director Georgina Dee

MIX
Paper from
responsible sources
FSC™ C018179
www.fsc.org

First edition 2002

Published in Great Britain by Dorling Kindersley Limited,
80 Strand, London, WC2R 0RL

Published in the United States by DK Publishing,
1450 Broadway, Suite 801, New York, NY 10018

Copyright © 2002, 2020 Dorling Kindersley Limited
A Penguin Random House Company
20 21 22 23 10 9 8 7 6 5 4 3 2 1

A CIP catalog record for this book
is available from the British Library.

A catalog record for this book is available
from the Library of Congress.

ISSN: 1542 1554
ISBN: 978 0 2414 0728 8

Printed and bound in China.

www.dk.com